Hot Potato

Understanding Why Children with Autism Spectrum Disorders Make Social Errors and How to Correct Them

Frances Collette

Hot Potato
All rights reserved
Copyright © 2013 by Frances Collette
Art copyright © 2013 by Denis Proulx

Interior Book Design and Layout by
www.integrativeink.com

ISBN: 978-0-9894314-0-8

No part of this publication may be reproduced, stored in a retrieval system, or transmitted in any form or by any means electronic, mechanical, photocopying, recording, or otherwise, without the written permission of the author or publisher.

TABLE OF CONTENTS

FOREWORD v

PART I HOW WE LEARN SOCIAL BEHAVIOR 1

    Learning Social Interaction 3

    Instincts and Instinctive Learning.. 7

    Social Insight... 19

    Understanding the Components 25

    Teaching Social Insight.. 35

    Social Errors.. 57

    Additional Considerations 69

    Changing Social Behavior 75

PART II LOOKING AT THE COMPONENTS 79

    Social Actions... 81

    Social Words... 87

    Social Signals.. 103

    Social Setting.. 117

    Social Sense.. 131

PART III TOOLS TO CHANGE BEHAVIOR 147

    Considerations for Changing Behavior 149

AUTHOR'S NOTE 161

GLOSSARY 163

FOREWORD

Many times parents of children with Autism Spectrum Disorders (ASD) shake their heads because their children fail to use common sense when dealing with social issues. Teaching social skills is one of the biggest challenges parents face with children with ASD. This book discusses how to teach social skills to children with Asperger's Syndrome, high functioning autism, and Pervasive Developmental Disorders who are able to communicate.

It is about ways to help children learn social rules and become more successful at home and in school. While most children seem to automatically know many social rules, other children need to be taught these rules. Unfortunately, the rules are not written down and most people don't even know they exist. Not only that - the rules change based on where you are, who you are with, and many other factors.

This book looks at the reasons that your children seem to lack common sense when it comes to social interaction. It discusses social instincts and instinctive learning, which is the way most people acquire social skills. As you come to understand this process, you will be better able to spot the reasons for your children's errors. Then you will be able to use this knowledge to teach them more appropriate behavior.

As an advocate, parents would describe to me behaviors that were causing problems for their families. I would work with them to find ways to change their children's behavior and make them more successful. These efforts were met with a high degree of success.

When parents asked me to put my ideas into a book, I began to think about a framework to communicate the principles I was using in devising behavior interventions. It took me a long time to figure out how to effectively translate my interventions into a simple formula – to help parents understand the reasons children with ASD respond differently than neurotypical children.

I developed the concept of Social Insight – with Social Actions, Words, Settings, Signals, and Sense – to act as a framework for these ideas. A framework offering a simple explanation for the reasons ASD children make mistakes and ways to correct these mistakes.

As a volunteer advocate, I worked with parents on a daily basis to help solve problems encountered by children with ASD. Once parents really understand why their children fail to learn some social behaviors, they are better equipped to teach them. Once parents know how to teach these behaviors, their children become calmer, more cooperative and more successful.

This book is separated into three parts. The first part of the book will help you identify and understand important issues related to learning social interaction. It is detailed and uses many examples. The next part discusses each of the components of Social Insight, giving specific examples for each aspect of behavior. It revisits many of the examples in the first part, explaining how these problems were resolved. The final part discusses the tools you can use to help your children learn to use Social Insight. All the examples reflect actual cases and the actual results of these interventions.

Everyone occasionally has a problem interacting with others. Some people even have frequent social conflicts, but still have friends and succeed in school or business. Individuals with ASD, however, often have major social issues that occur with a great deal of frequency. Their social problems often interfere with developing friendships and with their success.

The following chapters discuss practical ways to solve problems with social behavior and ways to teach your children to improve their own ability to understand social situations. Social Insight is a way of observing and thinking that will give your children the tools to make their own social judgments when confronted with unique situations.

Although all of the cases discussed in the book are based on actual children and their specific problems, in a few cases the stories are based on typical responses that have occurred over the years with many children with ASD. For example, problems with fire drills are so frequent that in any given year I may see more than one "Tommy."

If you come across an example that has affected your child, in most cases there is an explanation later in the book as to how the problem was resolved. However, I would encourage you to read through the entire book before beginning the process of teaching Social Insight to your children. Since later sections of the book discuss different aspects of these interventions, it is important to have read the entire book in order to be sure you are using the best approach and have the right tools.

I am writing this book to help your children be more successful in social situations. When they better understand social issues, they have a better chance to achieve their personal goals. Parents have frequently asked me to put my ideas into a book. I hope you will find them helpful.

PART I
HOW WE LEARN SOCIAL BEHAVIOR

LEARNING SOCIAL INTERACTION

By the time children are between two and three years of age, we expect them to have learned a whole variety of social rules. We are very patient with two-year-olds. We often find their social errors humorous, even when they embarrass us. As they get older, however, we become less patient.

▶ THE FAT LADY AND THE TWO-YEAR OLD

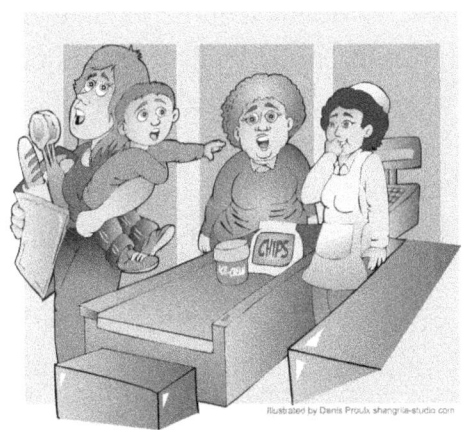

Imagine you are at the grocery store. Your two-and-a-half year old points to the next lady in line and says loudly, "Look mommy, fat lady." What do you do? I expect you would stammer an apology and, in a stern voice, tell your child, "Don't say that." Other shoppers might smile. Your reaction - immediate, intense, and unusual to this little one normally praised for clever words - signals that something different happened.

Once outside the store, you would give your child an explanation. You might say, "Don't say bad things about people," or "We don't say that people are fat." Typical children learn quickly.

Some children may learn the very first time to avoid negative comments in public; others may need several experiences before getting the idea. But for the most part, typical children understand what you mean when you say, "Don't say bad things." They do not need a formal explanation or a detailed list of subjects to avoid. They understand they should not say "bad things" about others out in public where they can be overheard. They understand that they can still talk to their parents about these things privately.

If you substitute a six year old in this example, the reaction of the other shoppers may be quite different. By that age, children are generally expected to have learned not to make loud, offensive public comments that can be overheard by the person being ridiculed. If a rude comment is made by a six year old, we might expect other shoppers to look at both the parent and the child with disapproval. The parent's embarrassment results in a more serious scolding and emphasizes the child's need to avoid this behavior.

A twelve year old making this comment would be considered extremely rude or odd. Shoppers would not just look with disapproval, but might make loud, offensive public comments that can be overheard by both the mother and child (Well! How Rude!). This public scorn is part of how a society eliminates unacceptable behaviors. Other people observing an event they find unacceptable may subject the offenders to ridicule for breaching a social norm.

Think how complex it is to learn what comments you can and cannot make. Very young children must judge if their comments are descriptive or offensive. They need to judge if another person is close enough to hear. They need to know that things they talk about with their family may not be okay to talk about outside the family. And, they need to learn when it *is* appropriate to make loud, offensive public comments. All these decisions must occur in just split seconds, before those fat ladies walk away from the checkout lines.

Yet, there are no lesson plans or books to teach this and other complex social skills. Most children simply learn these lessons by observing how those around them react. Children with ASD often do not learn this type of lesson in this way.

INSTINCTS AND INSTINCTIVE LEARNING

▶ INSTINCTS

We are born with instincts. Instincts are not learned; they are just part of who we are. When babies are born, they need to eat. Nobody teaches them what to do; they simply have an instinct to suck. This instinct was necessary for human survival.

Human beings have many social instincts – behaviors that are found in every human society. Anthropologists study the similarities and differences between cultures all over the world and note behaviors that appear in every culture, no matter how remote. They believe that some facial expressions are instincts.

> **Facial Expressions**
> **Blind children, who have never seen a face, have the same facial expressions for emotional states as other children do.**

Instincts require no learning. They are simply part of who we are. Your children may have problems because they lack some social instincts. Some children with ASD have a very limited range of facial expressions; others may have a wide range of facial expressions, but use them in an odd or inappropriate way.

▶ INSTINCTIVE LEARNING

When I talk about instinctive learning, I am talking about a process by which children learn certain skills and abilities without direct instruction. This is how the neurotypical two year old learns not to say bad things about fat ladies. Current theories suggest that we are hard-wired to learn some parts of our culture; that our brains are programmed to automatically learn what is socially appropriate. When someone fails to learn in this way, they may appear to lack common sense.

This learning is accomplished through observation and interaction. Social skills acquired through instinctive learning vary from culture to culture. They may include such things as how far away you should stand when speaking to a friend, where to look when addressing a person in authority, and how loudly you speak in various settings. Many people are not even aware these behaviors differ from culture to culture and even from group to group. They are part of the reason why some people feel uncomfortable when they are with an unfamiliar group.

> **Lying or Respect?**
> **When children are reprimanded by their teachers for bad behavior, they may look at the teacher or they may look away. In our culture, the children who look away are believed to be lying. In other cultures, the children who look away are showing respect.**

Children with ASD may have problems because they lack the ability to learn social behaviors instinctively.

▶ LEARNING SOCIAL SKILLS

Instinctive learning is the way most of us learned the majority of our social skills. We learned how to interact socially by observing how other people acted and intuitively used the same behaviors. Most of our skills were acquired without direct instruction.

The ability to instinctively learn social skills varies from child to child. It is not all or nothing. Typical children, as well as children with ASD, have different levels of ability. Even when children have trouble learning social skills instinctively, they can acquire some appropriate behaviors.

Social behaviors can be learned through trial and error, copying, guessing, and even chance. When your children are accepted, praised, or otherwise rewarded for using a correct social response, they will tend to repeat it. Unfortunately, because social requirements are so specific, this type of learning can lead to uncomfortable results.

Copying

One way to learn social behavior is to watch what other people do and then copy their behavior. In the case of copying, children are making a decision to use words or actions they have seen someone else use.

> ***Susan's Words***
> *When 10 year-old Susan meets a new girl her age, she often says, "Your hair is so beautiful. You are so pretty." Susan is copying what adults say to her, but her new acquaintance becomes uncomfortable.* [1]

Susan has learned this social skill by copying, but she does not realize that she is using words an adult uses with a child. They are not words a child can use with another child.

---
1 See Chapter Social Words

Social behaviors that are copied may or may not be successful. Susan selected a behavior she had seen before and continued to use it even though it was unsuccessful. She was unable to connect her lack of success starting a new friendship with the behavior she was copying. Other children might notice that the behavior they tried didn't work very well and try something new the next time.

Direct Instruction

Having typical social skills is partly instinct, partly a result of instinctive learning, and partly a result of direct instruction. Direct instruction is intentional teaching. It is the process you use to teach your children to tie their shoes or learn the alphabet. A simple example of social skills that result from direct instruction is manners. Manners are a set of rules that are intentionally taught; most people are aware that manners differ from group to group and that they don't just "come naturally."

> **Dinner Time**
> **What you do with various plates and utensils at a table is taught to you in childhood through direct instruction.**

▶ SOCIAL CHALLENGES

Social Interaction Issues

There are clear differences between the way children learn to interact socially and the way they learn language. When children have problems with language:

- **Age appropriate levels are clearly defined. Professionals take note of children's language and let parents know when their children deviate from accepted norms.**

- **Difficulties tend to be consistent across settings.**

These two important factors are not present when it comes to social skills:

- **There are no clearly defined parameters for social skill acquisition. In fact, there are so many different personality types that it is very difficult to pinpoint subtle deviations.**
- **Social skills vary dramatically across settings.**

How should your children's social skills be developing? The range of normal behaviors is very wide – including both shy children and boisterous children. Children's social behavior may be very different depending on where they are and who is present. Social experiences are so varied it can be difficult to decide when a real problem exists.

Often our children have better social skills at home. At home there have been many opportunities for repetition and direct instruction. Also, in some familiar community settings, such as the local McDonalds, children have close supervision and many opportunities for one-on-one demonstrations of what to do and say.

Even if children failed to learn instinctively, adults were present to give directions on "correct" behavior in these familiar places. Finding themselves in unfamiliar places, such as school, where no direct instruction on social skills occurs, the children may not be able to figure out what to do. Or, as often happens, they select the wrong behaviors.

▶ SOCIAL CHALLENGES IN SCHOOL

There are many reasons why serious social interaction issues become more obvious when children begin school. Let's look at how a social interaction problem may look in a school setting.

Hot Potato

On the first day of kindergarten, Mrs. Smith is teaching her new students to play Hot Potato. In this game, the children stand in a circle and pass a ball to the right while music plays. When the music stops, the child holding the ball is "out" and must sit down. One student, Johnny, does not want to stand near the other children and seems not to be paying attention. Mrs. Smith takes him by the hand and leads him to the circle.

Lily gets the "hot potato" and drops it. She is encouraged to pick it up and to pass it to Joey who is on her right. Joey takes the ball and throws it across the circle to Peter. The teacher sighs, retrieves the ball from Peter, and patiently explains that Joey must pass the ball to Sally on his right. When Sally gets the ball, she quickly gives it back to Joey. She does not want to have to sit down if she has the ball when the music stops. Again Mrs. Smith explains, Sally must hand the "hot potato" to Johnny on her right.

Johnny loves to play with balls. He will often spend fifteen or twenty minutes looking at a ball or an hour bouncing one against the side of his house. When Johnny gets the ball he is delighted. He promptly runs away from the group to sit under a nearby tree and look at it.

All hell breaks loose! The cheerful, patient Mrs. Smith begins to scream, "Come back here," but Johnny doesn't respond. She eventually reaches the tree and snatches the ball away from Johnny, who begins to cry. Determined that Johnny is a naughty little boy who must not "get his way" just because he cried, Johnny is put in time out as he begins to have a tantrum. Johnny's parents are called for a teacher's conference.

The real question here is why does Mrs. Smith cheerfully and patiently correct the other children's errors, but not Johnny's? In fact, Mrs. Smith actually punishes Johnny for his mistake.

When children hand the "hot potato" in the wrong direction or throw it to someone, the teacher realizes that they have not learned the rules of the game. She is comfortable helping the children practice and may even repeat the rules many times. When a child takes the ball and walks away from the group, the teacher does not even realize there was a rule.

When Johnny took the ball and ran away from the group, he violated a number of social rules. Johnny was supposed to know that a circle is a group and that you don't leave it unless you are out. He was expected to know the ball belonged to the group, even if someone gave it to him. He was expected to recognize his teacher's tone of voice and to look at her because the volume and pitch meant there was a big problem - all the other children were looking. And, finally, he was expected to know when his teacher raised her voice and yelled, "Come back here," that she was talking to him, even though she didn't use his name.

No one told Johnny he could not take the ball away from the circle, even if someone handed it to him! He was simply expected to know this rule. The actual rule is, "When you are playing a game with a group and a ball, you do not leave the group and take their ball." Think about it - where did all the other children learn this rule?

The understanding that the Hot Potato circle is a special type of social interaction is typically learned instinctively. The teacher knew that many children would not know the rules of the game Hot Potato; she did not know that some children do not know what it means to be part of a group. Because Mrs. Smith was never taught this rule, but learned it instinctively, she did not know that Johnny needed to be taught the rule.

How might a neurotypical child act in this situation if the child was from a foreign country and spoke no English at all? That child would not understand any of the teacher's words, but we can be pretty sure he would have followed the other children to the circle. When handed the ball, he would not have walked away with it. And he would have known there was a problem when Mrs. Smith used "the voice." When the teacher screamed, "Come back here," you can be sure he would have turned to look, riveted by her tone, though he did not understand a word she said.

When these types of misunderstandings occur, school becomes very stressful for children with ASD. They want to be successful and feel a lot of anxiety when someone is angry. When they are faced with unknown rules, they cannot predict the reactions their behavior will produce.

▶ TYPICAL BEHAVIOR MANAGEMENT

Since typical approaches to behavior management work so well with most students, when they don't work with ASD children the adults working with them tend to become very frustrated. Here in kindergarten, where Johnny is the most stressed he has ever been in his young life, the adults around him become impatient and angry.

Typical behavior management interventions which use rewards for "good" behavior and consequences for "bad" behavior usually have limited success. In many cases, they increase anxiety or eventually are ignored by the children who do not really understand what is expected. If they do not know which behaviors are good and which are bad, how can they earn rewards consistently?

Of course, not all children with ASD have the same level of difficulty with social understanding. A child like Johnny has a fairly high level of impairment. Other children on the spectrum may make errors that are more subtle.

It is pretty clear that Johnny's problem was not simply misunderstanding directions. He has failed to learn social behavior instinctively and will need a different type of instruction and special supports to be successful in school.

▶ ASD OR SOCIAL LEARNING

I have occasionally heard parents refer to social errors their children make as a part of their disability. With direct instruction, however, many inappropriate social behaviors can be corrected.

Carl's Response

Most of the time, Carl was a very verbal child; but, when his mother called his name, he did not respond. Mom knew Carl heard her and assumed his failure to respond was simply part of his autism.

I explained to Carl's mother that it was possible he simply did not know he was supposed to say something when he heard his name. After all, his mother had not asked a question or told him to do something. I suggested mom teach him to answer when she called his name. We chose the response "Yes?" and set up a reward system.

After explaining to Carl what he had to do, practicing with role playing, and reminding him, Carl soon began answering when his mother called his name.[2]

---

2   See Chapter Social Words

In this case, Carl simply did not know that hearing his mother say his name meant she wanted him to verbally respond. It wasn't that he couldn't respond; he just didn't know he was supposed to.

Anytime you shake your head and wonder about your children's social behaviors and find yourself thinking, "It's just common sense," you are probably looking at a behavior you learned instinctively. Think about it. If you had not learned instinctively, why would you act the way you do?

> ***Martin's Sounds***
>
> *Martin is an anxious, tense child. He becomes stressed very easily. In his second grade class, he has no friends. The teacher says that she has tried to encourage the other children to play with Martin, but the children don't want to. The teacher can't explain why the other children won't play with him.*
>
> *I asked the teacher if Martin makes noises or talks to himself. The teacher looked uncomfortable and said yes, he talks to himself.*[3]

Some teachers have a very hard time telling parents the reasons other children do not want to play with their children. In some cases, they see inappropriate behaviors as part of the child's disability and believe the behavior cannot be changed.

When teachers cannot explain why classmates reject children, I always ask if the children make noises or talk to themselves. It is not unusual to receive an affirmative response.

ASD children are often rejected by peers because of sounds they make. Many ASD children do not know that they can talk to themselves "in their head" without talking out loud and that they may have some control over the noises they make. It is important to attempt to teach any social behaviors your children need to be

---

3   See Chapter Social Signals

successful. If the instruction is successful, your children's lives will be enriched.

▶ PROVIDING SOCIAL INSTRUCTION

There is no profession focused primarily on teaching social behaviors. There is no college curriculum for Social Behavior Pathologists. We have many excellent professionals who do assist children to acquire social skills: speech/language pathologists, psychologists, behavior analysts and caring, creative teachers. Unfortunately, most available teaching materials focus on a few specific skills, rather than on establishing a broad understanding of social interaction.

There isn't even a highly developed, specific vocabulary to discuss social learning. Unlike language specialists, who have specific terms for even the most obscure aspects of language acquisition and use, there are few terms to discuss the finer points of social interactions.

How do parents, teachers, family, friends, and total strangers typically deal with ASD children's social mistakes? The range of responses is varied, of course, but rarely does anyone react by teaching a new social behavior. Even when parents try to tell their children what they should do, the correction typically occurs while the child is still upset or confused and is not treated as a lesson. Learning appropriate social behavior requires repetition, practice, and a positive learning environment.

SOCIAL INSIGHT

It is critically important for children to learn about the social world. Without some understanding, it is difficult for individuals with ASD to ever feel they have control over their social interactions. Without some understanding, their successes or failures are "hit or miss." Because it is impossible to teach every set of social behaviors, I would like to help you teach some general principles of social interaction.

My goal is twofold. First, I want to help you become aware of how you learned your social skills. The more you are aware of what you learned instinctively, the easier it will be for you to teach your children what they need to know. Second, I want to help your children develop what I call Social Insight. Social Insight is having enough understanding of social rules to judge how to act in new situations.

▶ COMPONENTS OF SOCIAL INTERACTIONS

It is possible to identify some components of social interactions and it is very important for your children to be able to identify them. I am using new terms to describe these components, using simple words to label some complex ideas. We are going to look at the what, who, where, how and why of the social world.

Social Actions and Social Words

Social Actions and Social Words are **what** happen during a social interaction. It is what we normally think of as social behavior - the general things we do. When you tell someone what happened at a party or what your child did at school, the Social Actions and Social Words are the main things you typically choose to relate.

Let's think about a play. Social Actions and Social Words are the parts of the script the director expects to see reproduced by each and every actor auditioning for a part. Social Actions are the stage directions required by the script. Social Words are the dialogue.

> **During an audition for a TV sitcom, the director asks the male actor to walk across the stage and take the hand of the female actor. The male actor says, "Would you go with me to a movie." The female actor looks at the male actor and smiles.**

At this point, you think you know what this scene is about. You have filled in some information based on your own background and preferences. But you really know very little. All of your information is based on the Social Actions and Social Words.

When teachers talk about problems your children are having, they typically describe the Social Actions and Social Words. This tells you very little about what happened.

Social Settings

Social Settings are **where** and with **whom** a social interaction occurs. It includes the place and the people. We will be looking at the factors that make up the Social Setting.

The Social Setting is the backdrop of the stage and all the actors. When the director holds an audition he selects actors who fit the scene he wants to portray. Consider our TV sitcom where the male actor takes the female actor's hand and says, "Would you go with me to a movie?"

If the male actor was a child and the female actor was a grown woman, you would have interpreted the scene very differently than if the male actor and female actor were both adults.

When the male actor approaches the female actor, you have a different reaction if they are in a typical living room or in the recreation room of a mental hospital.

We have different reactions to social situations based on where they occur and the clothing, age, race and other characteristics of the people involved.

When teachers speak to you about problems your children have encountered, you may want to ask about the Social Settings in which the problems occurred. It is not unusual that problems are specific to a particular Social Setting.

All children are routinely taught the behavior to follow in certain Social Settings. For example, you would tell your children ahead of time exactly what to expect and what to do at a wedding or a funeral.

As you learn more about Social Settings, you will be able to help your children remember to check the Social Setting before joining a group or entering a new situation.

Social Signals

Social Signals are **how** someone engages in social interactions. They include aspects of behavior that help us decide what Social Actions and Social Words really mean. Social Signals are not particularly subtle; we just don't think about them in the same way we think about Social Actions. We will be talking about how to help your children identify and use Social Signals.

The Social Signal is what a Director uses to communicate the deeper meanings of a plot. Let's look at how Social Signals work.

In one production of our sitcom, the adult male approaching the woman is well dressed, smooth and sexy. He looks "cool." You immediately anticipate a positive response.

In this case, the young man's Social Signals are telling you that he is socially appropriate and confident.

In another production, the same adult male approaches the same woman. Although he is well dressed, he is hesitant and appears nervous. His body is tense. He looks confused. You immediately anticipate a negative response.

In this case, the young man's Social Signals are telling you that he lacks some social skills and is unsure of himself. Your impressions are formed in a split-second.

Some Social Signals are understood through actual instinct – certain Social Signals are identical in every culture around the world. Other Social Signals are learned instinctively; we assign meaning to them because we have observed their use in our culture.

When teachers have difficulty describing why they have problems with your children or why other children avoid them, it is often because your children's Social Signals are odd or inappropriate. This is what happens with children who make noises. When you identify incorrect Social Signals and teach new Signals, problems are frequently resolved.

Once you learn to look for Social Signals, they are easy to spot and you will be better able to teach your children about them.

Social Sense

Social Sense tells us **why** we should behave in a certain way in a social interaction. Your children need to think about the reasons they are engaged in a particular social interaction. Social Sense can also tell us **why** other people are doing what they do. We will be looking at ways to help your children develop their Social Sense.

Johnny's difficulty in the Hot Potato game was a result of his difficulty with Social Sense. Even though he heard the rules, he did not understand his part in the game. He may not have even considered that the direction to "pass the ball to the right" applied to him.

Your children can use their Social Sense to determine if a current social interaction matches one they have already learned; or, in a unique situation, they may learn to use certain neutral responses. Problems with Social Sense sometimes are the basis for children with ASD reacting in unusual ways to what other children seem to take in stride.

Social Sense can be used to answer many social questions.

What do I do now? What do I say now? What is expected of me?

Once your children know to ask these questions, they will be well on their way to improving their social interactions. Once you understand these problems, you may be able to help your children become more successful.

Social Insight

Social Insight occurs when all the components fall into place. It is the **comprehension** that social interactions are made up of distinct parts that can be studied and understood at various levels. It is how we understand and implement unstated rules of behavior. We will be discussing how to help your children develop this insight.

Social Insight tells us to use our Social Sense to understand our interactions with others, to evaluate Social Settings and to carefully select Social Actions, Social Words, and Social Signals to achieve our goals.

When looking at the components of social interactions it is not always easy to fit everything neatly into one category or another. For example, reasonable people may disagree whether or not a particular behavior is a Social Action or a Social Signal.

As we look at various interactions, there may be disagreements about the "right" classification for some behavior. Because social interactions are multi-faceted, many times a behavior is both a Social Action and a Social Signal. Getting the classification right is not what is most important. What is most important is having the words to help you understand why your children are having problems and to help them understand more about social interactions.

UNDERSTANDING THE COMPONENTS

▶ SOCIAL ACTIONS AND SOCIAL WORDS

Social Actions and Social Words are the main parts of a story. They tell us what happened. We are usually quick to notice when someone is using the wrong Social Action or the wrong Social Words.

Choosing correct Social Actions can be difficult if you have not learned your social skills instinctively. When a teacher describes problems with your children, Social Actions and Social Words are the main part of the story. In many cases, teachers assume that children who behave inappropriately either have bad manners or are trying to be disruptive or defiant.

Ethan at School

A very bright student, Ethan was having a hard time adjusting to his new middle school. He went along with his mother and me to a teachers' meeting. As we began the meeting, Ethan sat on the classroom floor. He remained there through the meeting. I learned that Ethan also sat on the floor when he visited the counselor's of-

> *fice, causing other students to think he was strange. Ethan almost always sat on the floor at home.*[4]

At home, it is just fine for children to sit on the floor for most activities, but Ethan had never learned that this Action might not be appropriate if he was not at home. Mistakes about appropriate Actions and Words can create some very serious problems. It is very important to help your children learn what Social Actions and Social Words are appropriate in various settings.

Social Words also present many challenges. Sometimes our children use the wrong words and sometimes they misunderstand the words we use.

> **Kenny's in Trouble**
> *Kenny is extremely literal and uses words according to their dictionary definitions. Kenny believes a liar is anyone who says something that is not true. When a student at school answers a question incorrectly, Kenny calls him a liar and gets in trouble.*[5]

Kenny was using the dictionary definition of lying – saying something that is not true. When he calls another student a liar he gets in trouble because he doesn't understand the Social Meanings of words.

▶ SOCIAL SETTING

The Social Setting is often the most critical component when deciding which Social Actions and Social Words are appropriate. Where you are and who is present can change everything! Without

---

4   See Chapter Social Action
5   See Chapter Social Words

awareness of the Social Setting, otherwise acceptable behaviors can prove disastrous.

> **Daniel's Movie Date**
> *Daniel was in eighth grade and had no friends, but he was getting along great with Mike. In their Tae Kwon Do class they would work on routines and joke around. Daniel wanted to see if Mike would go to the new Chuck Norris movie with him.*
>
> *After class, as Mike talked to his girlfriend, Daniel walked over. He asked Mike for his phone number so he could call him to go to a movie. Mike turned away from Daniel and avoided him from then on.*[6]

If you are unsure why Mike turned away from Daniel, consider the Social Setting. Remember, Social Setting includes where you are and the people who are present. Daniel did everything right except he didn't consider that Mike's girlfriend was present. He had asked another teenager for his phone number to go to a movie in front of the teenager's girlfriend!

Daniel could have asked Mike for his number and said he needed a ride to school or to get together to practice Tae Kwon Do; but, in front of Mike's girlfriend, Daniel asked to go to a movie – a typical dating activity. Mike was embarrassed in front of his girlfriend.

Had Mike been alone and Daniel made the same request, I doubt there would have been a problem. Actually, if Mike had been with his mom or dad, I doubt there would have been a problem. The outcome depended on Mike's relationship with the other person to whom he was speaking.

Misreading a Social Setting can sometimes be disastrous. Mike's rejection of Daniel was devastating and this encounter raises many issues. Parents whose children have suffered rejection are often angry and bewildered at the cruelty of others; but those issues are

---
6   See Chapter Social Setting.

not in the scope of this book. I want to help Daniel learn how to avoid this type of rejection in the future.

But how could this have been avoided? We will be talking about helping your children to evaluate Social Settings.

▶ SOCIAL SIGNALS

Social Signals add meaning to our Social Actions and our Social Words. Let's take a look at how Social Signals work.

An example of the problems caused by not understanding Social Signals frequently occurs in our children's classrooms.

Cindy's Upset

Cindy sometimes came home very upset because she was in trouble at school. Cindy said her teacher yelled at her for talking and sometimes she would cry herself to sleep. Each time her mother talked to

> *Cindy's teacher, the teacher was baffled. Cindy was a model student and never "got in trouble."*
>
> *Cindy's teacher told me there were other students in the class who were scolded for talking. I asked the teacher to demonstrate how she corrected them. Mrs. Smith looked where the students would have been sitting and said in a stern voice, "Stop talking." When the teacher corrected other students, Cindy became distraught. Cindy thought the teacher was talking to her!*[7]

Cindy did not recognize the Social Signal the teacher gave by looking at the students she was correcting.

This is actually a very common problem. When group leaders are correcting members of a group, they frequently use eye contact and do not use names. Because many of our children do not understand Social Signals, they do not understand that these reprimands do not apply to them.

Social Signals arise in many different settings. The following incident describes how Social Signals are both sent and received.

> ### A Friend's Visit
>
> *When my friend Danny visited from out of town, he wanted to attend an Overeaters' Anonymous meeting with me. He belonged to a small group in his hometown and wanted to visit the larger group in Miami.*
>
> *When it was time for members to speak, Danny raised his hand and went first. His talk was "different." He talked about his serious emotional problems and detailed descriptions of each meal he ate*

---

7 See Chapter Social Signals

the previous week. He moved his arms and hands in wide, agitated gestures.

While Danny was talking, members of the audience began to shift in their seats, roll their eyes, and looked at their watches. Danny was asked to sit down before he was finished speaking.

Danny is incredibly bright. In fact, his IQ test scores show him to be a genius. He learns entire computer languages by simply reading through a book once. I asked him why he thought he was asked to sit down. He said that in the group he attended in New York everyone was allowed to speak for five minutes; since this group was larger, he thought he must have gone over their time limit.

I asked Danny why, when the audience became restless, he had not ended his talk quickly. He wondered what he would have seen or heard to help him know that people wanted him to stop talking. I demonstrated by shifting in my seat, rolling my eyes, and looking at my watch.

Danny was also surprised to learn that he should have listened to some other speakers and tried to make his talk fit the group. I explained he could have listened to the topics they discussed, noting how personal or detailed they made their remarks, the types of gestures and movements they used, and, finally, how long they spoke. He felt he could have made his talk similar if he had known.

After I demonstrated and explained these Social Signals to my friend, he said, "Well, now that you've told me, I'll never forget." And, he never will.

▶ SOCIAL SENSE

Social Sense helps us have success in social interactions. We must know why we are involved with others before we can make good choices and we must know the special rules that apply to different interactions. When your children understand why they are engaged in social situations and understand the special rules for different times and places, they can be more successful.

Unfortunately, some people with ASD are not even aware when they are part of a social group. They may define relationships differently. They may not understand that when they are with a group of people, at least some of the time, they are part of the group.

Johnny's unfortunate experience with Hot Potato is just one example of problems caused by a lack of Social Sense. If Johnny had been taught the rules of being part of a game he would have had a better chance of being successful.

Your children first need to learn how to identify when they are part of a group; then they can begin to figure out their role in that group.

> ***David at the Blackboard***
>
> ***The whole class was working at the blackboard when Mr. Jones announced, "It's time to sit down." All the students returned to their seats except David. Mr. Jones repeated loudly, "It's time to sit down." David did not move. Again, more loudly, Mr. Jones said, "I SAID, it's time to sit down NOW." David continued to work at the board!***
>
> ***Now angry, Mr. Jones walked toward David and said, "David, I've told you three times to sit down!" As David walked to his seat, he looked directly at Mr. Jones and said, "Once."***

From David's point of view, since he was only addressed by name once, he had only been asked to sit down once. And, while there may have been a number of different reasons for David's behavior, one of the problems was that he did not see himself as part of a group. When directions were addressed to the group, he did not understand that he was always included. Despite being very intelligent, he lacked Social Sense.

▶ INCONSISTENT BEHAVIOR

Some ASD children behave appropriately some of the time. In fact, some of the time they seem just about perfect! When this occurs, the good behavior is used as evidence that inappropriate behavior is intentional. Of course, all children intentionally misbehave some of the time, but with our children it is often harder to tell.

In some cases, children with ASD have learned how to be "good." In school, for example, they know when they sit still and do their work they will not get in trouble. Through trial and error, they have identified a limited range of Actions, Words and Signals they can use to avoid negative consequences.

Unfortunately, these children may not know what to do when they are not "on their best behavior." When there are new demands or when they cannot sustain perfection, their behavior may become inappropriate. Changes in behavior aren't always due to a decision to act up or break rules; sometimes our children simply do not know what behaviors to use when they are not being perfect. Sometimes children who are otherwise very well behaved melt down into major tantrums when they are overwhelmed.

In school, something as simple as another child asking to borrow a crayon or bumping on line might trigger behavior that is disruptive. A common trigger is having a substitute teacher who changes the class routine or uses words differently than the child's regular teacher. When a change in behavior occurs, there is always a cause; but, it can be a real challenge to track it down.

When ASD children's behaviors change, we need to be very careful in imposing consequences. Consequences have no meaning if children do not know what they did wrong or if they are unable to control their behavior. Consequences for bad behavior usually have limited success. In many cases consequences increase anxiety or frustration and make a difficult situation worse. If ASD children do not know what behaviors are "good" and what behaviors are "bad," consequences have no meaning.

▶ RELATED ISSUES

Helping children improve their social understanding and their behavior is often complicated by a number of other problems. Children with ASD often have problems with attention, frustration tolerance, anxiety, hyperactivity, obsessive/compulsive needs, cognitive abilities, tics, overstimulation, sensory issues, and many other things. All of these factors may interfere with their ability to comply with our instructions.

When teaching Social Insight these related issues must be taken into consideration. We must be sure our children are able to do what we ask them to do.

TEACHING SOCIAL INSIGHT

To most of us social learning came effortlessly. It just made sense. Learning social rules, even rules that seem simple to you, may be very, very difficult for your children. Many times, teaching a rule will require many repetitions, practice and even role playing. You may have to answer many, many questions and repeat the same lesson many times. Your children are not trying to give you a hard time; they are struggling to understand something that is very difficult for them.

A good analogy, for most people, would be trying to learn Algebra. Even though you were given formulas and rules, you had to repeat the same lessons over and over before you learned! You needed a quiet place to study and a lot of practice. Social rules are just as hard for ASD children.

Hopefully, your children will become better able to understand the various parts of social interactions with careful instruction. When they have a framework with which to think about how to achieve their social goals, they will be on their way to having Social Insight.

Translating instinctive learning into a normal day to day teaching process can be challenging. Because we did not learn our social behavior this way, it is easy to overlook teaching opportunities. But, with practice, you will be able to help your children.

When we teach our children about social behavior, we need to be able to clearly identify Social Actions, Words, Signals and Settings. We need to translate unstated social rules into simple rules our children can understand and follow. This is how they will develop their Social Sense.

For example, your children may be very literal. They may interpret the statement "sit quietly" to mean sit without talking or sit without making sounds. They may not think it means not to move around, not to play with the dog, or not to toss a pencil in the air while the teacher is talking. You can, however, teach your children the Social Meaning of phrases like "sit quietly."

We can also give our children ways to identify if their behavior fits a particular Social Setting. We can show them how people act differently in different Settings and teach them to watch what other people do. Once they understand what to look for, what Social Actions or Social Words are being used, they have a better chance of being successful.

They can learn in a new Social Setting to do only those things others are doing if these are things they are allowed to do. By routinely talking about the behavior your children observe, they learn more about how to act.

Social Signals are more difficult to learn than Actions and Words. Many Signals have meanings that are instinctively learned - while you can see and hear Actions and Words and describe them accurately, it is very difficult to describe many Social Signals. Our children can be made aware of Social Signals, however, and practice using them. Social Insight develops as our children learn that these Signals exist and that they can learn their meanings.

▶ EVERYDAY LEARNING

Opportunities to learn about social behavior occur every day. As you share information about what you see, your children are learning. It is the same as any other learning, except you are talking about different things. You tell your children about things other children understand instinctively. Parents and teachers can point out Social Actions, Words, Signals, and Settings. Discussing social interaction can be a normal part of your day.

When my children and their friends were in the car, I would ask what they thought about different people we saw outside the car.

> **If a man was jogging at a comfortable pace going in the direction of the Metrorail Station, we decided he was going to catch a train.**
>
> **If a man was running very fast carrying a package and looking back over his shoulder, we decided he may either have stolen the package and was running away; or, someone might be chasing him to try to steal it.**

I would explain the difference between someone running very fast and someone jogging comfortably. I would explain how looking back means the person is looking for something or someone behind him. We would talk about possible reasons for what people were doing. I would point out that we were just guessing, but that having a theory about the people around us helps us understand the world.

This is a good, fun way to develop Social Insight. Whenever you can, point out Social Actions, Words, Signals, and Settings. Talk about why people may be doing what they are doing to help your children develop Social Sense. Even if your children with ASD fail to participate, they are at least being exposed to Social Actions, Words, Signals, Settings, and Sense on a regular basis.

I never realized how much this game and other discussions had influenced the children until one day when they were in middle school. One of the children told his mother how he avoided a fight because he stayed away from a new boy. Why had he stayed away from the new boy? He said it was because the new boy had "weird hair," a middle school Social Signal of defiance and possibly aggression. He had picked up a Social Signal all by himself!

This type of learning can also be used to correct behavior mistakes. Just remember to present the information when your children are not distracted and can give you their full attention.

Derek's Hugs

At the age of ten, Derek made several new friends in the neighborhood. The boys were about two years older than he was. He really liked his friends and he occasionally hugged them.

His mother told him that hugging was how their family showed they liked each other, but boys do a high five or pat each other on the back. She told him to watch what the other boys did and tell her about some of the things he saw so they could select the best way for him to show his friends he liked them.

What Derek was doing was not wrong, but it was inappropriate. His friends did "boy things" to show their friendship. Derek's errors were probably tolerated because he was younger, but if he didn't learn the "correct" Social Action, he would run into trouble later.

Derek was used to watching people because of frequent Everyday Learning opportunities. He saw what his friends did and checked with his mom to be sure he was selecting the correct Social Action to show he liked his friends.

You can explain simple mistakes to your children using these types of lessons. When they say or do something socially inappropriate, point it out and suggest other Social Actions, Words, or Signals. Sometimes you can tell them right at the time of a problem. Other times, you may want to wait until you have their full attention - but not too long after the mistake. You'll have to see what works best for your children.

Some of the brightest children with ASD are academically advanced for their age and speak like adults. Their errors are sometimes accepted as part of their intellectual strength. Many times they copy adult behavior. When this happens with adults, it may be looked at as charming. When this happens with other children, they are rejected.

Jerry's Greeting

When seven year old Jerry greeted someone, he would extend his hand for a handshake. Adults were usually delighted, but other children thought it was strange. Mom told Jerry, "Sometimes you need to do things differently when you are with children and when you are with adults." She told Jerry

to greet other kids by just saying "hi" and not by shaking hands. Jerry followed this new direction.

One of the problems that can get your children in trouble at school is that they may not know what "sit quietly" means.

You can practice at McDonald's, making it a game. First you sit quietly; then your children sit quietly. Remind them to stop eating while sitting quietly. Remind them not to wiggle or play with a toy while they are sitting quietly. Young children should enjoy this, including your neurotypical children. Show you are pleased when your children succeed.

It is important to introduce new behaviors as soon as you notice a problem, remembering to wait until a time after the incident when your children can focus. The more your children engage in the wrong behavior, the harder it is to change. Even though you may have to make the same suggestion more than once, with time your children may begin to remember to use the new behavior.

Most young children consider their parents to be very smart and are likely to accept their directions without question. It is important to start when your children are young so they are in the habit of following your suggestions. Once puberty sets in, it is less likely that your opinions on these types of issues will be accepted.

There are also many types of behavior problems that can be solved with this type of instruction. Where incorrect Actions, Words and Signals are caused by misunderstanding what is expected or what is appropriate, Everyday Learning can change behavior.

Opportunities for Everyday Learning occur all the time. Whenever our children make mistakes because they lack information let them know the right way to respond. It is not enough to say, "Don't do that anymore," you need to show them what they are supposed to be doing. If you are not sure if a problem can be corrected by using Everyday Learning, go ahead and give it a try.

▶ BEHAVIOR LESSONS

When Everyday Learning hasn't worked, you can try a Behavior Lesson. To change a behavior you need to:

- **Identify the social errors, including any Social Sense issues.**
- **Develop a Behavior Lesson.**
- **Teach the Behavior Lesson.**

Identify the Social Errors

Because children with ASD do not learn their social skills instinctively, it is up to us to try to help them develop these skills. We need to teach the actual social rules. But first, we have to figure out which unwritten social rules our children did not understand. The more rules they can learn now, the more successful they can be later.

When your children make mistakes, first decide if the errors were due to incorrect Social Words, inappropriate Actions, or badly chosen Signals. Sometimes Social Actions, Words, or Signals that would have been appropriate in another place or time become a problem because of the Setting. By focusing on specific errors, rather than an incident as a whole, it is easier to identify the problem. Social Sense mistakes have occurred when there are errors with Words, Actions, or Signals.

Initially, it may be difficult to identify social errors. We are not used to figuring out why a behavior is or is not appropriate. With time and patience, however, you will find that this may become easier.

▶ DEVELOP A BEHAVIOR LESSON

Once you have determined the social error, a Behavior Lesson may be obvious. Sometimes, however, it can be difficult to figure out. Social behaviors are infinite, so there are an unlimited number of errors that may occur. Each Behavior Lesson is unique to its error, but patterns do appear. When a Behavior Lesson works to correct one error, you know similar lessons will correct other similar errors. But remember, since some children with ASD do not generalize, a Behavior Lesson may need to be specific to one Setting. Then, if the same behavior appears in another Setting, a new Behavior Lesson may be needed.

All Behavior Lessons require a Replacement Behavior and an explanation of Social Sense. A lesson may also include a Reminder and a Reward. Finally, Teaching Time must be carefully planned for a time when your child is receptive and able to learn.

Replacement Behavior - What to do
Social Sense - Why you do it
Reminder - Help remembering to do it
Reward - Incentive for doing it
Teaching Time - Learning to do it

▶ TEACH THE LESSON AND PROVIDE SUPPORT

Behavior Lessons are more specific than Everyday Learning. They can either teach new behaviors or eliminate unwanted behaviors, but they incorporate very specific components. Behavior Lessons require both a clear description of Social Sense and a Replacement Behavior to "take the place" of the unwanted behavior. A Behavior Lesson may also include a Reminder, a Reward, or both.

Behavior Lessons also differ from Everyday Learning because they require a period of instruction, which I call Teaching Time. Your children must fully understand what is expected and demonstrate the ability to comply.

Because Behavior Lessons are used for situations that require a period of instruction, you should only address one or two behaviors at any given time. It is similar to learning math. You would not try to teach both addition and subtraction at the same time. Even in separate lessons, the new concept wouldn't be introduced until the first concept was mastered.

Behavior to Change

One reason ASD children get things wrong is that they don't know the right things to do. Even if children have gotten in trouble for making mistakes, they often repeat them. They either don't understand what they did wrong or they don't have another behavior to use. Behavior Lessons are designed to change or eliminate specific behaviors or build new behaviors. Once a lesson is taught, it must be practiced.

> *Jimmy's Running*
> *Jimmy is a whirlwind of energy. It is very hard for him to sit still, especially in his car seat. When he gets out of the car, he often takes off running. As hard as mom tries, sometimes she can't stop him.*

The most important part of a Behavior Lesson is to identify the behavior you want to change. Jimmy's mom wants to stop him from running away when he gets out of the car. He even does this in parking lots, putting himself in danger of being hit by a car.

Jimmy's mother will have to translate Jimmy's running away into an acceptable behavior Jimmy can master. The Lesson is to teach a new behavior to replace the old behavior, because completely eliminating a behavior is often too difficult.

Replacement Behaviors

Replacement behaviors are substitutes for behaviors that need to be changed. When your children do not know what to do, they may use the wrong Social Actions, Words, or Signals. ASD children may have unique sensory or physical needs and a Replacement

Behavior can give them a safe, socially acceptable way to feel better and still behave.

> **I suggested mom teach Jimmy to run in place right next to her.**

We selected a behavior very similar to the behavior Jimmy's mom wanted to change. Wherever possible, choose a behavior that is similar, but socially acceptable. This makes it easier for your children to make the transition to the new behavior.

Replacement Behaviors must be chosen carefully. They have to be Social Actions, Words, or Signals your children are able to do. It really helps if your children like the new behaviors or, at the very least, do not dislike them. Sometimes you can ask your children for suggestions for Replacement Behaviors.

If you are unsure if your children have the ability to do a Replacement Behavior, or if your children resist doing it, have them practice before you teach their Behavior Lesson. If they are unable to use the behavior you have picked, you will need to find a different Replacement Behavior.

Jimmy's Replacement Behavior is running in place; Carl's Replacement Behavior was answering his mother when she said his name - it replaced not answering.

Social Sense

Our long term goal is to help our children develop Social Insight. When they better understand their social world, they can be more successful. To do this, we need to give them as much information as possible about why we want them to do certain things. Remember, Social Sense tells us the reason we use certain Social Actions, Words, or Signals.

> **Mom explains to Jimmy that she would like him to run in place next to her when he gets out of the**

car seat. She tells him he could get hurt if he just runs off without asking first.

Even though Jimmy's mother has yelled at him many times for running off, he does not seem to understand he could get hurt. This time his mother is calm and gets him to talk to her about running. She helps him focus his attention.

Rewards

When you show your children that you are pleased with them or your children are excited about their own success, this is a reward. When Jerry greeted other children by saying "hi" instead of shaking hands, his parents were pleased and Jerry also got a better reaction from the other children. For Everyday Learning, this is all the reward you need. For many Behavior Lessons, however, rewards need to be more specific.

Rewards can be anything that your children like.

Children who are obsessed with Star Wars, and don't like anything else, cannot be effectively rewarded by going to a class prize box that has no Star Wars toys. Sometimes "rewards" don't work because the rewards that are offered have no meaning for children with ASD.

> **Jimmy really liked running in place and learned right away. He enjoyed practicing running in place and he liked that his mom was happy.**

In some cases, the Replacement Behavior itself is the reward. When Jimmy runs in place next to his mom, the running is a big part of his reward. His other reward is that his mother is happy and lets him know it.

Other behaviors, especially those that require new learning or that are difficult, may need more clearly defined rewards.

Teaching Time

You cannot correct a persistent problem behavior or teach new Social Actions, Words, or Signals, unless your children are receptive. Social learning is hard for them. Imagine trying to learn algebra in the middle of a County Fair or after you've had a car accident. Select a time when your children are relaxed - not right after they've had a problem.

Jimmy's mother decides to try the new behavior before Jimmy's swim class. Jimmy loves his swim class and always runs from the car when they arrive.

> **Two days before swim class, mom told Jimmy he would run in place next to her before his next swim class. For two days, they practice getting out of the car seat and running in place.**

Most social instruction occurs spontaneously amid chaos and calamity. Typical peers can be given a look or instruction and behavior is modified. The interaction occurs wherever and whenever an offending behavior occurs.

This frequently does not work for children with ASD. If your children become upset when you are teaching their Behavior Lesson, help them relax. If necessary, try again at another time.

Teaching Time must include interaction with your children. In this case, Jimmy is practicing his Replacement Behavior by running next to mom. In many cases, role playing is effective. Practicing a Replacement Behavior and providing explanations help your children understand what is required.

Repeating Behavior Lessons many times is just as important as practicing the multiplication tables. In both cases, you are using repetition to help your children remember difficult, new information. It is important for your children to actively engage with you during Teaching Time.

Reminders

In many cases, Reminders are critical to the success of Behavior Lessons. Even though you have gone over the Lesson many times, your children may forget and revert to previous behavior patterns. A Reminder right before they need to use the new behavior helps them remember what to do.

> **As mom pulled up to swim class, Jimmy was very excited. Before he got out of his car seat, she reminded him that he was going to run in place next to her when he got out of the car.**

When Jimmy's mother told Jimmy before he got out of his car seat to run in place next to her, she was using a Reminder. Jimmy ran next to mom and she let him know how happy this made her.

The Reminder must happen just before the new behavior is to be used. Even though you are sure your children have learned the Behavior Lesson, in the excitement or confusion of the moment, they may forget. It is not that different from reviewing spelling words right before a test.

In routine situations, you may not need to use a Reminder more than once or twice. After that your children may use their Replacement Behaviors without Reminders. When your children are excited or distracted, however, they may always require a Reminder. This is especially true when sensory needs are involved, as for Jimmy.

Older children can have parts of their Behavior Lessons written out and they can read their Reminders.

> *Roy's Reminder*
>
> *Roy made loud, rude remarks when other students or teachers made mistakes in class. His plan was to either silently write down his comments or think them in his head without talking. This part of his plan was laminated and put in his notebook to read every day. Roy liked reading his Reminder and told his teacher it was better than a counselor.*
>
> *When Roy got annoyed in class, he looked at his Reminder. Roy's remarks stopped. After a year, he took the laminated plan out of his notebook. He said he didn't need it anymore.*[8]

Reminders help our children remember their instructions at the appropriate time. They can help them remember what to do.

In many cases, if you have followed the steps above, and your children's behavior has not changed, there are problems with either the Replacement Behaviors themselves or the words being used to describe the Replacement Behaviors. For example, Roy was not just told to think his comments, he was told to think his comments without talking. While this might be obvious to you, it might not be obvious to Roy.

▶ UNIQUE LANGUAGE USAGE

Our children make several unique types of errors with language. One error is caused by a literal understanding of words. The

---
8 See Chapter Social Words

words are understood correctly, but our children follow the literal meaning rather than what the speaker intended.

Another type of error is caused by either adopting a unique meaning for a word or accepting only one meaning when a word has multiple meanings. I call these Mislearned Words.

Finally, there are the Social Meanings attached to words we use to discuss behavior. School rules and directions frequently fall into this group. Your children get into trouble because they honestly have no idea what is expected.

Literal Language

The language issue you have probably heard about is being too literal. This occurs when children hear an expression such as, "It's raining cats and dogs," and run to the window to look. When you give directions to your children and they don't follow them, it isn't that hard to figure out if they are following the literal meaning of the words you spoke.

> ***Paul's Water***
>
> ***When it's time for Paul's class to get water after recess, the teacher tells them, "It's time to go to the water fountain." All the children except Paul line up. Paul walks directly to the water fountain, cutting in front of the line.*** [9]

It is clear why Paul made this mistake. The teacher told him to "go to the water fountain." While Paul's classmates responded to what the teacher meant, Paul responded to what the teacher said. While Paul's teacher could change what she is saying, Paul would not be learning the Social Sense that he needs to be successful. Paul can be taught what the teacher means when she says, "It's time to go to the water fountain."

---

9   See Chapter Social Sense.

Mislearned Words

This type of error is also very frequent, but it is harder to figure out.

> *Dwayne's Touching*
> *Dwayne's sister began to yell, "Don't touch me." "I'm not touching you," he said. As Dwayne's mother got ready to lecture him to stop, he turned to her, poking her with his elbow, and said, "Right mom, I'm not touching you if I'm not using my hands."*

Although Dwayne knew his sister was annoyed with his behavior, he thought she was being unfair because she accused him of "touching" her. Without his comment, his mother would never have known to explain that touching included any body part coming in contact with something else.

> *Charles's Boinking*
> *Charles knew not to hit other children; but, one day, he hit another child for no apparent reason. It turned out that a group of first grade boys had been playing a game "boinking" each other. They would boink by hitting each other. Charles insisted that he had not hit his friend; he had boinked him. Charles was suspended from school for two days.*[10]

It is fairly common for some ASD children to learn to follow a rule only for a specific word. So when Charles learned not to hit, he did not apply that rule to a boink. Even though a boink was the exact same Social Action as a fairly forceful hit, Charles saw it as different because the boys gave it a different name.

Our children do not only mislearn single words, they may mislearn the meaning of a group of words or even a general idea.

---
10   See Chapter Social Words

Bob's Promise

Bob's mother was scheduled to pick him up at the babysitter's at six o'clock. If she was late, he would tantrum. Sometime he would cry, "You promised, you promised." Tired and guilty for being late, she tried many times to comfort him and explain why she was late that evening. Nothing seemed to help.[11]

In this case, Bob had mislearned the general idea of being "picked up at six o'clock." He took the time as an absolute - as a promise. While he was fine with getting picked up early, when he wasn't picked up by six o'clock he became agitated. Bob needed to learn that a general statement was not an absolute, not a promise.

When I was writing this chapter, I searched for a word in our language to describe this phenomenon. Try as I might, I couldn't find one and made up the term Mislearned Words. As you deal with errors your children make, you will probably find some examples of Mislearned Words.

Social Meanings

Social Meanings seem to become a much bigger problem once children with ASD enter school. Teachers use phrases such as "be quiet" without realizing that some children may not understand what is expected.

Social Meanings in School

We tend to speak in a type of shorthand which works pretty well for most people. We instinctively learn the group of behaviors that are expected for certain words and phrases.

---

11   See Chapter Social Words

> *Ryan at School*
> *Ryan is forever getting in trouble at school. His teacher says when she tells him to pay attention he ignores her. He frequently puts his head down or looks out the window. Ryan does all his work and always knows the answer when his teacher calls on him. Nevertheless, his teacher insists he needs consequences for not paying attention.*

What teachers often mean when they tell their students to "pay attention" is to sit up without speaking or fidgeting and to keep their eyes on the teacher. The literal meaning of "pay attention," however, is to focus your thoughts on something.

It is pretty clear that Ryan is, in fact, paying attention. His teacher is frustrated, however, because he does not look like he is paying attention. The Actions and Signals that Ryan's teacher associates with paying attention are not being displayed.

Many classroom rules and instructions fit this category. Ryan's teacher also has a problem when she tells him to be quiet.

> *When Ryan's teacher tells him to be quiet, Ryan doesn't say a word. Ryan wiggles in his seat, tosses his eraser in the air, or plays with a toy. Ryan's teacher says that he is disrespectful.*

It may seem obvious to you that Ryan should not be doing all those things, but he really is being quiet. "Be quiet" literally means not to make noise. Ryan is not making noise. This problem frequently arises when we are trying to teach our children appropriate behavior.

Social Meanings in Social Stories

When adults try to explain to children with ASD not to say hurtful things, they may use words that have Social Meanings that our children simply don't understand. The following is an actual paragraph that was provided to a child with ASD by an autism support teacher.

> **Sometimes I say things which can hurt or insult others' feelings. I sometimes need to express my feelings and thoughts and that is OK. I will express these feelings and thoughts with a safe person. Using put-down or demeaning language is not OK.**[12]

When this student was asked if he understood what he was supposed to do he answered "yes," but does that mean he really understood? Even if he could give a dictionary definition of each term, it does not mean he could identify these components in a real world context. When he again made a comment that was a put-down, this student once again got in trouble.

What words make something a put-down? What words are demeaning? If you do not understand how another person thinks, how can you determine if what you are saying will hurt or insult them?

In each of these cases, the problem is the same. Understanding the words Ryan's teacher uses or whether something is a put-down or demeaning depends on knowing the Social Meaning of the words.

▶ WHEN YOUR CHILDREN REGRESS

ASD children, just like neurotypical children, tend to become stressed if they don't feel well. They may become irritable if there are even minor changes in their normal routines. The illness of a parent, marital problems, a new pet, even an exciting vacation plan, can change their ability to behave. At school, being teased,

---
12   See Chapter Social Words

getting an "F" on an assignment and especially a new behavior management system can cause behavior changes and regression.

One common problem is when your children's schools have fire drills.

> *Tommy's Terror*
> *Tommy had an amazing first week at kindergarten. He came home each day happy and wanted to tell his mom about everything he did. But, when he came home on Friday, he was shaking and upset. He didn't want to go back to school.*

When Tommy's mother talked to his teacher, she learned the school had had a fire drill. Tommy had screamed when the fire alarm sounded, covered his ears, and refused to leave the classroom. It can take a long time to correct the damage done by fire drills.

Another common problem is when your children are not picked up at their usual time. They may become frightened and upset, especially if they are unprepared for this.

> *Fred's Tantrum*
> *Fred had improved so much. For many months, he had not had any tantrums and followed school rules. Until Monday morning when he told his mother he didn't want to go to school anymore. Once there, he was completely out of control: refusing to do his work, running from class, and screaming.*[13]

The last day Fred was in school, his sitter was late picking him up. He had to wait in the office for half an hour, something that had never happened before. Now he was afraid to go back to school.

---

13   See Chapter Social Sense

When there is a drastic change, try to think of everything that happened right before the change in behavior. If something out of the ordinary happened, especially something unpleasant, you have probably found the cause. Once you know what caused the change, it is possible to help your children recover and return to better behavior.

▶ CHILDREN WHO FEAR SCHOOL

Some ASD children are very, very good in school. At home, however, they are absolutely terrified and beg their parents not to take them to school. Some cry loudly and painfully in the morning before going to school and resist in any way they can. They may cry themselves to sleep at night fearing the next day at school.

There can be a variety of reasons for this to happen. Bullying is one and teachers who yell at their classes is another. Children may show their unhappiness in school by acting out or by having their grades go down.

When fear of school is caused by a behavior system at school, the situation often gets more complicated. Your children seemingly transform as if by magic when they walk to their classroom doors. What their teachers see are quiet, compliant children.

Parents who try to get assistance from their children's schools for school related anxiety frequently run into disbelief. Administrators and teachers listen to the parents pleas, look at their composed children, and wonder what is wrong with the parents. In fairness to the schools, it is very hard for school personnel to imagine the anguish of the parents and children with this problem.

> *Billy's Fear*
> *Billy had a wonderful year in kindergarten. When he began first grade, however, the teacher had a new behavior plan. If the children were good their behavior marker was on green. If they*

started to have a problem, it changed to yellow as a warning. And, if the marker was moved to red, they were "in trouble."

Billy now seemed to be stressed when he went to school, but Billy's marker was always on green. Then one day when there was a substitute, she moved his marker to yellow because he had not finished his work on time. From that day forward, Billy began to fear school.

At school he was perfect, but at home his fear grew worse and worse. Billy would cry and beg not to go to school. He would struggle not to get out of the car to walk to class. But, as soon as he saw his teacher, his behavior completely changed and he walked quietly into the room.[14]

In all the cases I've worked on with this pattern, the problem has been the behavior management system used in the children's classrooms. Any type of behavior management system that introduces the threat of "getting in trouble" can trigger this response, but the green/yellow/red system noted above seems to be the worst.

Sometimes there are meltdowns at school, but for the most part these children exhibit all their fear and anxiety at home. There is no solution except to change the behavior system.

---

14 See Chapter Social Sense

SOCIAL ERRORS

Many social errors are not random. They result from choosing the wrong Social Actions, Words, and Signals. What others learned instinctively is a "hit or miss" situation for your children. You will be able to help them more when you can identify their errors. Understanding the reasons for certain mistakes makes them easier to correct.

By putting errors into categories, what seemed to be random, or even bizarre, can now make sense. As your children become aware of their errors and the reasons they made them, they have a chance to avoid related errors in the future. When you explain their errors using categories of behavior, your children develop their Social Sense and may learn to ask questions before they do something new.

When parents and teachers recognize an error that falls into a certain category, it is easier to correct. Many of these errors can be corrected with Everyday Learning, just as Jerry easily learned not to shake hands with other children. Some are more difficult to correct.

I have selected the following categories because the problems they cause are very common. This is by no means a complete list.

▶ HOME VS. OUTSIDE THE HOME

Quite a number of inappropriate social behaviors can be traced to this category. These errors result from misunderstanding Social Settings.

Each family has its own rules about how to act at home. Some behaviors are allowed and some are not. Many home behaviors are not appropriate outside the home. You already met Evan who did not know the rules for sitting on the floor were different at school and at home.

A more serious problem arises for children who do not understand that home bathroom rules differ from school bathroom rules. If this occurs, it is usually when children with ASD first enter school.

> **Timmy's Toileting**
>
> **Timmy's kindergarten teacher called his parents for a conference. They were surprised when the school's principal and psychologist were at the meeting. It seems Timmy refused to close the door when he went to the bathroom and that he would walk out of the bathroom with his pants down. He would have a tantrum when his teacher yelled at him to get dressed. They wanted to refer Timmy for tests to determine if he had emotional problems.**[15]

Unfortunately, I have run into this problem a number of times where family rules allowed or even required their young children to leave the bathroom door open. In some cases, they were encouraged not to dress themselves until a parent was called to the bathroom. The families of children who have trouble with toileting, especially problems cleaning themselves or engaging in creative play in the bathroom, are likely to have these rules.

Neurotypical children from families with these rules know the school rule is to keep the bathroom door closed. They know when they leave the bathroom at school they must have all their clothes on. No one has to tell them. Our children do not always know this or may be unable to use different rules in different set-

---
15   See Chapter Social Actions.

tings. Because many ASD children are not flexible, correcting this problem quickly always requires changing the family rule.

A very unfortunate incident occurred with a high school student I'd worked with for several years. While his mother and I met with his teachers and his counselor, Joe found a way to loiter outside the room. Joe's mother went into the hall to encourage him to return to class.

> ***Joe's Kisses***
> ***Joe hugged his mother. He kept his arms wrapped around her as she spoke to him quietly and he kissed her on her cheek. He pleaded with her to take him home and not make him go back to class. His actions were observed by other students. When Joe did go back to class, he was ridiculed by his classmates for "making out" with his mother.***

Neither Joe nor his mother realized that this loving behavior, perfectly acceptable at home, was not appropriate in a high school hallway. The social damage from this incident affected Joe for the rest of the school year.

▶ FAMILY ONLY

This refers to behaviors you may engage in only with your closest family members, whether or not you are at home. Like problems of Home vs. Outside the Home, these problems have to do with the Social Setting. In this case, however, it is the people not the place that is the problem. These rules are vitally important not only to avoid serious social problems, but also for safety.

Deciding who constitutes close family differs for different families. Once you decide who to include, all you need is a list. I've found that our children do not have a very hard time with this once it is explained.

> **Karen's Cuddles**
> **Ten year old Karen cuddles with her dad and sits on his lap. She may put her hand on his stomach or his thigh and she wiggles around. When Uncle Harold visited from out of town, to his embarrassment, Karen sat herself down on his lap and began to cuddle.**[16]

Uncle Harold quickly removed himself, but he was uncomfortable during the entire visit. Karen seemed hurt and confused.

The issue wasn't where Karen was, but who she was with. It could have happened at a picnic or during a car ride. Even worse, it could have happened in a place or at a time where she would not have been safe.

Now aware of Karen's difficulty understanding relationships, her parents became ever more vigilant. They have made lists of her family and "close family" and private parts. They review the lists frequently to be sure Karen understands.

They have taught Karen she must always tell her parents if someone touches her in any place on the private list, even if she tells someone she won't tell. They teach her that any promise not to tell does not include her parents or her doctor.

▶ PRIVATE BEHAVIOR

ASD children need to be taught from a very young age that certain behaviors should only occur when they are alone. While these behaviors fit more than one category, our main concern here is with their effect as Social Signals.

---

16   See Chapter Social Setting

When your children are little, an exception can be made for parents, but even brothers and sisters should not be included. In most cases, normal family patterns may need to be modified, so the "only when you are alone" rule applies to all family members.

One of the reasons it is so important to teach this early, before your children enter school, is that these behaviors can become habits that are extremely difficult to change. Another reason is that errors on private behaviors cause severe social problems.

Adrian's Self-Talk

Adrian was an excellent student in fifth grade. He enjoyed following directions and doing his work. He was never considered a behavior problem, but he frequently talked to himself. While the teachers liked him, they found the self-talk distracting and children in the class avoided him. They thought he was strange. At home Adrian also talked to himself.[17]

---

17   See Chapter Social Signals

Adrian learned not to talk to himself out loud in a relatively short period of time. Once his parents set up a Behavior Lesson, it took him about three weeks to stop.

Adrian could engage in self-talk in his room when he was alone, but not when anyone else was present. Yes, he would occasionally forget, but when reminded he was able to control his self-talk.

I first heard the term self-talk a number of years ago. Some people now believe that self-talk is simply one of the symptoms of ASD. Once again we see a behavior that seems to be part of a diagnosis that in many cases can be changed.

Some private behaviors should only be allowed when your children are alone in their rooms or in a closed stall in a bathroom.

> ***Frank's Nose Picking***
> *Twelve year old Frank is bright, does well academically, and has relatively good social skills. But, Frank does not have any friends. Throughout the day, Frank picks his nose.*[18]

Frank's parents have tried periodically to help Frank stop picking his nose. Unfortunately, by the age of twelve, this is a very difficult habit to break. Selecting a Replacement Behavior is difficult, especially because some ASD children with sensory issues do not like the texture of tissues. The sooner the behavior is redirected, the less likely it is to become a habit.

In the worst cases, errors on private behaviors may be interpreted as sexually deviant.

---

18   See Chapter Social Signals

> **Sean's Crotch Massage**
> **When nervous, Sean rubs his crotch. His middle school teachers tolerated this behavior; they thought it was part of his disability. Sean's first week in high school, he was suspended and threatened with expulsion for deviant sexual behavior.**

Like Frank, Sean has a habit that is not socially acceptable. Not only did this deprive him of friends, but it put him in jeopardy at school. While his suspension was resolved, he needs to change this habit. Sean could be arrested if he does this in a public place.

The problem of teaching private behavior is complicated by our popular culture. The rappers crotch grab is one that comes to mind. Neurotypical children know how to copy this, while concealing their behavior from supervising adults - just like they know how to conceal when they pick their noses.

Your children need to avoid private behavior in public. Severe problems may result if they do not.

▶ HOW WE TOUCH

You likely had some direct instruction on how to touch other people. For example, you were probably taught how to shake hands or how to hold a dance partner. Rules also exist for day to day physical contact, although you may not even realize it.

> **William Gets Jill's Attention**
> **William and Jill sit next to each other in school. They are good friends. One day, Jill was looking down at her work and William touched her face to get her to turn around. Jill got upset and William got in trouble with his teacher.**[19]

---

19 See Chapter Social Action.

Poor William was very confused; he really hadn't done anything wrong. He had not hurt Jill. Even so, just because he touched her face, he was in trouble.

If you touch someone in the wrong way, you can get in a whole lot of trouble. Tap your boss on the shoulder to get his attention, no problem. Tap your boss on the nose to get his attention, big problem. Tap the office secretary on the butt to get her attention and you may get fired for sexual harassment.

Getting a social greeting even slightly wrong can make people feel uncomfortable.

> ***Denis' Air Kiss***
> *Denis is pretty good at following social rules, but one day he got into a discussion with his mom about the brief hug and kiss of a greeting. He thought the kiss was on the cheek with the lips. His mother explained it was cheek to cheek with an "air" kiss. He didn't believe her until he confirmed it with a female friend.*

As your children get older, they tend to trust their friends' judgments on social issues more than their parents' judgment. If they are fortunate, they will have helpful friends. Because Denis' friend confirmed he should use an air kiss, he changed his behavior.

Unfortunately, wanting to be accepted and fit in can cause our children to have problems.

> ***The Bra Snap***
> *In Todd's middle school, the boys have a new game. They are "snapping" the girls' bras. Some of the girls think it's funny and Todd wants to be*

> *in on the fun. He snaps Sally's bra, but he does it right in front of his teacher.*

Once again, a child with an ASD gets in serious trouble. Had Todd known that he was not allowed to touch someone's underwear, even through their clothes, there is at least a chance he would not have snapped Sally's bra. But it is unlikely anyone would have thought to give him this rule.

How and where you touch another person varies from culture to culture. For your children, it is best to set strict guidelines. No one will be too offended if you touch them only in the right places, or even not at all.

▶ THEORY OF MIND

Theory of Mind refers to the ability to understand what someone else is thinking. We do this all the time. Neurotypical people are constantly modifying their behavior based on the reactions they get from other people. We observe reactions and modify what we do because of subtle social cues. We can usually distinguish an uncomfortable reaction from an encouraging reaction.

Making judgments about the reactions of others is very difficult for individuals with ASD.

> *Teasing*
>
> *Jason has begun sitting with his sister and her friends in the cafeteria in middle school. His sister is upset because Jason makes mean remarks to her friends. Jason insists her friends find his remarks funny because they smile. He doesn't believe his sister when she explains they are actually upset.*

Smiles create huge challenges for ASD children. Even in social skills groups, they are taught that a smile means someone is happy or likes them. In the real world, a smile can mean that someone is laughing at you because you are being inappropriate or that they are masking their own discomfort.

▶ UNKIND WORDS

When I talk about unkind words, I am talking about the type of words your children say without malice or anger - words that may make other people feel badly. They are often factual statements or a repetition of something your children have overheard.

> *Tina's Comments*
> *When Tina is at school, she often makes comments to other students. She might mention if someone has a new dress or a haircut. One day Tina told another student she smelled bad. The teacher reprimanded Tina for being rude and called her parents for a conference.*[20]

To Tina, this was just another factual statement, but the teacher believed Tina made the remark on purpose to be mean. How can your children tell the difference between a factual statement they can say and a factual statement they should not say? In most cases, all you need is a list.

> *Philip's Racial Slurs*
> *Some of the boys at Philip's middle school are into Gangster Rap. They listen to rap music and copy the styles and words used in music videos. Philip wants to be part of their group and tries to*

---

20 See Chapter Social Words

act like them. Philip was called to the principal's office for using the N word to another student. Philip insists that he did nothing wrong.

What Philip doesn't realize is that there are a whole set of Social Signals that notify his classmates when it is acceptable to use these types of words with their friends. Absent those Signals, this language is always offensive.

▶ CORRECTING SOCIAL ERRORS

Because your children do not learn their social skills instinctively, many do not understand what they can and cannot say. Even if they are upset when someone is rude to them, they may not realize when they are being rude to others.

Because these lessons are difficult, our children may need to actually study what is and what is not appropriate. Very specific guidelines may be required so they know the words and actions they can use and the words and actions they need to avoid.

ADDITIONAL CONSIDERATIONS

In addition to not learning social skills instinctively and having challenges with language, many children with ASD have other problems that affect their ability to be successful.

They may be identified as suffering from attention problems, impulsivity, low frustration tolerance, sensory overload, or cognitive problems. You may have been told they have an anxiety disorder, obsessive compulsive disorder, oppositional defiant disorder, or a thought disorder. Your children may also have health problems such as allergies, asthma, seizures, or tics.

In order for your children to change their behavior, they must have the ability to do what you want them to do. Even if they want to do what you ask, they may not be able to comply. It is our job to develop Everyday Learning and Behavior Lessons our children are able to follow.

The following list mentions some of the more common issues to consider. The list is certainly not exhaustive, but may be helpful.

▶ ATTENTION

Without your children's attention, you can't get to anything else. If your children are not paying attention, their lessons cannot be learned. How well your children can pay attention may vary from day to day. If they are sick or they are upset, it is more difficult for them to pay attention. It is easier for them to pay attention to preferred tasks than to things that do not interest them.

You may be able to help your children improve their attention through various techniques. For example, you can integrate special interests into activities your children do not normally prefer or you can give rewards at frequent intervals.

▶ AUDITORY PROCESSING

Even a child who has taken a hearing test and passed can have an auditory processing problem. Children with this problem are not always able to understand what is being said to them. They may be unable to understand words in quiet places even if there is just a little background noise.

Think about when you are washing dishes at the sink and the water is running. Even though you have normal hearing you may need to turn off the water to hear what someone is saying to you when they are only two or three feet away. This is one example of how a child with an auditory processing problem might experience voices when there is background noise.

Auditory processing problems often do not become an issue until your children are in school. In a classroom, the sound of the air conditioner or even a chair moving can make it hard for children with this problem to understand what their teachers are saying. Background voices can also create problems in classroom settings. An auditory processing problem may look like an attention problem.

Auditory processing problems are really quite common for children with ASD. If your children have normal hearing, but turn up the sound on the television when there is a little bit of noise in the room, consider checking for an auditory processing problem.

▶ COGNITIVE MELTDOWNS

Some children with ASD experience cognitive meltdowns. When I use this term, I am talking about children who actually lose the ability to understand directions when they are upset. They are not really able to process what you are saying to them or what you want them to do once in a meltdown.

In working with children who experience this type of meltdown, it is especially important to identify what I call the "rumbling" phase - the behaviors you observe before the full meltdown occurs. It is very rare that our children do not exhibit some sign before a cognitive meltdown, although the signs can be very subtle. It is important to find a way to step in before the full meltdown occurs.

▶ SENSORY CHALLENGES

When I refer to sensory challenges, I am referring to how children's bodies function and how that impacts their ability to be successful. All children are affected by how they feel. Children who are hungry or sleepy are not as receptive or as cooperative as children who are more comfortable.

Children who need movement may benefit from standing up to do their lessons; children who need pressure may benefit from squeezing or lifting heavy objects; children who are sensitive to sounds may need to be protected from noisy environments; and, children who become overwhelmed may need to learn deep breathing.

The needs of children with ASD are very varied. If there are problems that cause children physical distress, these problems must be addressed in any plan to change behavior. It is difficult for children with sensory challenges to be successful without addressing these needs.

▶ INVOLUNTARY SOUNDS AND MOVEMENTS

Involuntary sounds and movements may include facial movements, such as moving the nose as if sniffling; head, limb or body movements, sometimes in a sequence; or noises including grunts or squeaks. These movements may be completely involuntary and your child may or may not be aware of them.

For children with certain medical diagnoses, these movements may be called tics. But some ASD children make these sounds and movements without a diagnosed medical condition. While children sometimes have some level of voluntary control for short periods of time, for the most part these sounds or movements are involuntary. When working to address Social Signals, it is important to keep in mind whether your children are able to control the Signal you are trying to change.

▶ MEDICAL PROBLEMS

Some ASD children also have medical problems. If your children are sick, they cannot be expected to perform at their best. When you are aware of medical issues, it is important to take them into consideration in developing a Behavior Lesson. It is not uncommon for children who have been doing very well to regress when they are feeling ill.

▶ SPECIAL INTERESTS

Some children with ASD develop special interests. These interests may be age appropriate or they may be unique. What sets special interests apart from typical interests is the intensity with which your children pursue them. Even children who typically have a hard time paying attention may be able to spend extended periods of time attending to a special interest.

In some cases, you can use your children's special interests to help them maintain interest in something you want them to do or to learn.

CHANGING SOCIAL BEHAVIOR

When I first begin working with a family, I help them decide which problem behavior or behaviors they want to work on first. Because this learning is difficult, your children cannot be expected to learn too many things at one time. While in some cases there is only one behavior that has brought a family to contact me, most of the time there are several problems.

Because changing behavior is difficult, I recommend that you never try to change more than one problem behavior at a time. Changing a behavior may require learning more than one Replacement Behavior and it is important that your children are not overwhelmed.

When there are many problems, I look for the Social Actions, Words, or Signals that are having the greatest impact on the family's and the child's wellbeing. In many cases, parents feel the behavior is obvious, such as a "tantrum." But, selecting a behavior is very specific. You cannot use a general concept to correct a specific behavior.

To change a tantrum requires specific knowledge of the Social Actions, Words, and Signals involved. For example, some parents describe their children's tantrums as crying loudly for three or four minutes while sitting or standing in one place. Some parents describe their children's tantrums as thrashing on the floor for forty-five minutes, screaming, throwing objects, biting and kicking. These two "tantrums" are very different events, requiring very different interventions.

When teachers say that children are disrespectful, for example, I want the teacher to break this down into Social Actions, Words, and Signals. You need to be able to see what happened - to make a mental picture.

It is not unusual that a parent will report an incident where a teacher said their child was rude, but the parent has no idea what actually happened. Because we are not used to describing actual behavior, we use terms that have Social Meanings, but fail to communicate actual events. When trying to decide what behavior to change, try to consider what you or others have actually seen or heard.

Ask questions that must be answered with descriptions of actual Social Actions, Words, and Signals.

- **What did you see my child do when he was not paying attention?**
- **What did my child say or do that made you feel he was rude?**
- **What does my child do when you ask her to sit quietly?**
- **Can you describe an incident that made you feel my child was disrespectful?**

Ask yourself these questions about things you have seen your children do that you felt were wrong. See if you can figure out which Social Actions, Words, and Signals made you feel that way. After a series of very specific questions, you will be better able to determine what actually happened.

▶ CAN A BEHAVIOR BE CHANGED

Before putting Behavior Lessons in place, it is important to figure out if the behaviors are in your children's control. The good news is that many behaviors can be changed. Even those that are not completely voluntary may be controlled to some extent. In some cases, children learn to delay behaviors until an appropriate time.

Some behaviors are involuntary. These behaviors result from physical conditions and cannot be changed. Seizures cannot be voluntarily controlled nor can some tics. Children cannot be taught to correct problems with balance or coordination. While this seems obvious, it is not always easy to figure out if a particular behavior is voluntary or involuntary.

Some seizures look like children are simply staring, giving the appearance they are not paying attention. Some coordination problems appear when children are tired or stressed and may look like they are just acting silly. Some tics look like children are intentionally making faces or noises.

There are also behaviors that result from physical conditions that need to be addressed before the behavior can be changed. Children who are sick or who are extremely fatigued cannot be expected to change their behaviors without addressing their physical needs. This comes up fairly frequently with children who are sleeping in class. Children with sensory issues must have their needs met either through therapy or sensory breaks before their behavior can change.

PART II
LOOKING AT THE COMPONENTS

SOCIAL ACTIONS

Social Actions are the things people do. They are what we normally think of as social behavior. When you tell someone what happened at a party or what your child did at school, the Social Actions are a major part of the story. We are usually quick to notice when someone is using the wrong Social Action.

Choosing correct Social Actions can be difficult if you have not learned your social skills instinctively. When your children use the wrong Social Actions they may look odd or seem to have bad manners. In school, your children may get into trouble when they select the wrong Social Action.

Problems that result primarily from a lack of information are usually easy to resolve. Many situations, however, are more complex. Your children may have to replace an incorrect behavior pattern.

Behavior Lessons are used when the learning involved in changing a behavior requires information and practice. There can be physical, emotional, or other factors contributing to behaviors that need to be changed.

Many different things happen in a classroom: raising your hand, doing work at a desk, talking with other children, class parties, and so on. For most activities there is no actual instruction; it is assumed that students know what to do. In school, walking on line can present challenges for children with ASD. How close or how far it is appropriate to walk can cause problems unless the proper distance is explained.

> **Sarah Stumbles**
> When Sarah was on line, she would stand very close to the child in front of her. She would bump into the child when the line stopped moving and might trip over the other child's feet while they were walking. Sarah's teacher yelled at her to "keep her distance," but Sarah did not seem to understand.

After determining that this behavior was not caused by physical issues, it was easy to resolve. Once Sarah's problem was explained to her teacher, the teacher showed Sarah how to hold her hands out in front of her to leave space between her and the child in line in front of her. The problem was easily solved with this Everyday Learning lesson and a short period of practice.

Many children with ASD run into problems with Social Actions that are part of being in school. If they learn a behavior incorrectly, it can lead to problems. Unlike Sarah, Mary did not really understand why she should walk on line. She had somehow come to believe that it was her job to be the line leader.

> **I'm Line Leader**
> Mary is very challenged in kindergarten. Many things seem to overwhelm her and any transition or change is difficult. When the class lines up, Mary becomes agitated, repeating over and over, "I'm line leader, I'm line leader." If she cannot be line leader, a tantrum may ensue. If she is not line leader, she becomes upset each and every time the class lines up.

Brainstorming with Ms. Arnold, Mary's teacher, I suggested that Mary might not understand what it means to be "on line." Repeating, "I'm line leader,"

LOOKING AT THE COMPONENTS

might be her way of telling herself what to do, a kind of Reminder. We decided to give Mary a Reminder she could follow herself.

Ms. Arnold sat with Mary one-on-one and explained that beginning the next day Mary would walk on line with the other children. She told Mary that many children took turns being line leader and when she was not line leader she would walk on line. Ms. Arnold showed Mary how you walk on a line - facing forward, hands at your sides, and not too close to the child in front of you.

Ms. Arnold told Mary that when she walked on line she would repeat, "I'm on line. I'm on line." Mary's teacher practiced saying "I'm on line" with Mary and they walked around the room saying, "I'm on line." Ms. Arnold praised Mary for how well she walked on line and for saying, "I'm on line."

The next day, Ms. Arnold asked Mary's mother to bring Mary to school early. They practiced walking together saying "I'm on line," and Ms. Arnold praised Mary. When it was time to line up, Ms. Arnold prompted her to begin repeating "I'm on line" over and over. She then walked with Mary to her place in line and walked along with her repeating, "I'm on line; I'm on line."

After a week of practice, Mary was walking in line by herself, repeating "I'm on line."

In this case, Mary had learned the wrong Social Action. She had learned that when she walked from class to class she would be the line leader. No one had tried to teach her the correct Action using an actual lesson.

Simply telling Mary that she should walk in the line, or scolding her when she didn't, did not work. In addition, Mary needed a

Reminder. Mary's Replacement Behavior was walking on line; her Reminder was first the teacher saying, "I'm on line" and walking next to her; later she herself would say her Reminder, "I'm on line."

The Replacement Behavior was extremely similar to the behavior we were trying to change. It is unlikely trying to get Mary to walk on line without the repeated phrase would have worked.

Ethan at School

Ethan was having a hard time adjusting to his new middle school. He went along with his mother and me to a teachers' meeting and sat down on the classroom floor. I learned that Ethan also sat on the floor when he visited the counselor's office, causing other students to think he was strange.

Ethan's mother felt he could easily understand there are different rules at home and at school, but this issue was more complicated. Since children also sat on the floor at school, Ethan needed guidelines to know when this Social Action was appropriate at school.

His mother spoke to him at home one evening when he was relaxed. She told him there were different rules for what people do at home and what they do in other places. They talked about things that are different at home and at school. They also talked about some of the things you do in both places.

She told Ethan he was allowed to sit on the floor at school only if a teacher told him he should or if other students sat on the floor first. She attempted to repeat the discussion again before Ethan went to bed, but he told her he understood the new rule.

Ethan's mother asked his teachers and counselor to let her know if he again sat on the floor inappropriately at school. It was not reported that he had any further problems.

Ethan's problem arose because sometime the rules for Social Actions can become complicated by where you are. There were times when it was appropriate for students at Ethan's school to sit on the floor. When a teacher was late to class, students would sit on the floor to wait. Because sitting on the floor was part of the school's culture, it was important to help Ethan know when he could sit on the floor at school.

While this could also be considered a Social Setting problem, I am treating it as an example of a Social Action problem because sitting on the floor was sometimes allowed at school.

SOCIAL WORDS

Problems caused by language errors show up in many different ways. They can be caused by children following literal meanings, using adult language, failing to respond when they hear their names, and many other errors. The shared characteristic is that these problems are caused by Social Words.

The younger your children are when you teach them about Social Words the easier it is to avoid problems. As with many issues, once a behavior pattern is established it is more difficult to change. The best way to teach these Words to your children is to simply tell them what words to use and what different words mean.

One of the saddest situations arising from misusing words is rejection by peers. While these types of rejections are usually the result of many factors, if your children are not using children's words it can contribute to rejection.

▶ CHILDREN'S WORDS

Because children with ASD do not learn their social skills instinctively, they may not realize that children and adults use different forms of communication. This was the problem that Susan experienced when she tried to make friends.

Susan's Words

When 10 year-old Susan meets a new girl her age, she often says, "Your hair is so beautiful. You are so pretty." Susan is copying what adults say to her, but her new acquaintance becomes uncomfortable. [21]

Susan's mother decides to use Everyday Learning to teach her there is a difference between children's words and the words adults say to children. Before she talks with Susan, she prepares a list by listening to other children and asking Susan's brothers.

Susan and her mother usually read together every evening. Before reading, her mother explains there is a difference between the way children talk to each other and the way adults talk to children. She gives Susan examples and asks if she can think of any.

Susan's mother has written down adult comments she remembers Susan making around girls her age. She has also written down the words she has collected from other children. When Susan's mother explains there is a difference between how adults and children talk, Susan is very interested.

Mom tells Susan when she meets new children she should use children's words. For a little while they role play. Sometimes Susan plays the child, sometimes mom plays the child. Together they try to think of other things adults and children say differently. Mom tells Susan she is going to ask one of Susan's cousins if they got the words right.

Her mother tells her what a good job she is doing thinking about choosing children's words. Susan

---
21 See Chapter Tools to Change Behavior.

begins to use her new words more and does a little better interacting with other children.

It is important to use real children's language. For example, "Hi, how are you today?" is only a little better than what Susan was already saying. If you are not sure what comments work, ask some neurotypical children; or, better yet, try to listen to actual conversations. These lessons can continue in a relaxed way indefinitely, as part of Everyday Learning.

▶ UNKIND WORDS

Sometimes your children may hurt other people's feelings or say things that seem very rude. At least some of the time, it is because they do not understand when a comment is hurtful.

Because ASD children have difficulty understanding Theory of Mind, they don't know what other people are thinking. They may be unaware when they are saying something hurtful. Even children who have been upset by unkind words from others may not understand what could make someone else feel badly.

> ***Tina's Comments***
> ***When Tina is at school, she often makes comments to other students. She might mention if someone has a new dress or a haircut. One day Tina told another student she smelled bad.***
>
> In talking to Tina about why she got in trouble in school, her mother explains even true statements can make another child feel badly. Tina and her mother talk about comments that will make someone feel good and comments that will make someone feel badly. They use very specific examples.

Tina's mother has prepared a list with some of the rude comments she has heard Tina make. The list includes some unkind things she has heard Tina say to other children and to her brothers; it also includes mean things Tina's brothers say to her.

She also writes down some appropriate comments she has heard Tina make. Tina's mother tells her she should not use the words on the list that make someone feel badly except when she talks with her parents or her safe person at school.

She also talks with Tina about times at school when she hears other children say things that are unkind. She explains that even though other children may say these things, Tina should not say them.

Tina's mother also realizes that sometimes when Tina and her brothers interact, they say things to each other that are not kind. She sits down with all of her children and explains which things they say are okay and which are not. She tells them from now on when they say unkind things to each other she will point it out and make them to stop.

At first, Tina's mother reviews the list each day after school and adds things that Tina says she hears other children say. They continue to talk about nice things to say. Eventually, Tina becomes able to understand most of the time which facts are not nice to say.

To Tina the fact that a classmate smelled bad was just another factual statement. How can your children tell the difference between a factual statement they can say and a factual statement they should not say? You simply have to teach them.

These types of lessons are usually very effective for children who can't judge when a factual comment is unkind. Some children must learn statement by statement, while others may be able to learn general rules. As they become more aware of the effect of language, they typically learn to make better judgments about what statements are "nice" versus "not nice."

The meeting with Tina and her brothers is very important. Tina's neurotypical brothers know not to say the mean things they say to Tina to their friends. When parents hear their children making nasty remarks to each other, the usual reaction is to simply tell them to stop. Rarely does a parent stop to review what was said and why it is not allowed. It may be necessary to actually prohibit this type of interaction at home in order not to confuse or upset your ASD children.

One of the biggest problems with this lesson is the "cool kids" at school. They often say really mean things to each other but remain very popular. I find it interesting that some ASD children are able to identify the popular kids.

When our children see popular children acting in a certain way, they sometimes try to copy the behavior. If this happens, it is usually best to simply explain that while others might talk in this way, your children should not. Will that work? Only some of the time, but it can't hurt to try.

▶ MISLEARNED WORDS

Mislearned Words create serious problems. They are also among the most difficult of the problems with Social Words to identify.

> *Charles's Boinking*
> *Charles knew not to hit other children; but, one day, he hit another child for no apparent reason. It turned out that a group of first grade boys had*

been playing a game "boinking" each other. They would boink by hitting each other. Charles insisted that he had not hit his friend; he had boinked him. Charles was suspended for two days.

When Charles got home from school he was very upset. He felt his teacher was unfair. His mother waited until he had calmed down and had rested for a while. When she was sure he was calm, she explained that when one child strikes another child with force, it doesn't matter what you call it. Whatever name you give to that Action - whether a "hit" or a "boink" - if the Action is the same then the same rule applies.

Mom also did some role playing with Charles. She told Charles to "boink" her softly on the arm; then she told Charles to "hit" her softly on the arm. She showed him that what he did each time was exactly the same. She explained it was the Action that was against the rules, not what it was called.

Charles protested. He said all the boys boinked and they didn't get in trouble. His mother explained that children get in trouble at school when someone who enforces rules sees what they did or is told what they did. She explained if the teacher did not know another child was boinking, he could not get in trouble. She explained if the teacher knew other boys were boinking they would also get in trouble.

The next two days - the days Charles was suspended - his mother repeated this lesson several times. Each time Charles seemed to understand a little better what he was being told. When she took Charles to school the next day, she reminded him about the rule before he went to class.

It is an important Social Sense concept that it is the Action not the Word that is the basis of a rule. Charles did not get in trouble again for any type of hitting. And, although he still got in trouble occasionally for breaking other rules he did not fully understand, he had learned an important lesson about rules.

Bob mislearned what a promise was. He believed a statement that something will happen is a promise. Because Bob has mislearned what a promise is, his mother must teach the difference between a promise and a plan.

Bob's Promise

Bob's mother was scheduled to pick him up at the babysitter's at six o'clock. If she was late, he would tantrum. Sometime he would cry, "You promised, you promised." Tired and guilty for being late, she tried many times to comfort him and explain why she was late that evening. Nothing seemed to help.

On Friday night, mom sat down with Bob before he went to bed. She explained that a promise is special and that it requires the person making the promise to actually say it is a promise; she explained a plan is something we want to do, but that it may be changed without a discussion.

She talked with Bob about some things that had been promises - to go to the zoo on his birthday or to visit his grandfather. They talked about other promises and agreed that Bob will check with his mother if he thinks something she said was a promise.

His mother also explained that even if something is a promise sometimes things happen to make it impossible to do what was promised. She explained that if she promised to go to the zoo on his birthday, but it rained very hard, they might have had to change the promise and go another day. She explained that even a promise can be changed, but that they will talk about it before they change a promise.

Finally, Bob's mother explained that when she says she will pick him up at the babysitters at six it is a plan not a promise. She reminded Bob about traffic jams and flat tires and having something extra to do before she can leave work. Bob tells about things that have happened to him that made him change his plans - like when he planned to clean his room but had to watch a favorite show instead.

Bob's mother initiated and repeated this discussion twice on Saturday and again twice on Sunday. By this time Bob was telling his mom that he "got it" and she should leave him alone. On Monday, before she dropped him off at school, she reminded him that she "planned" to pick him up at the babysitters by 6 o'clock.

For several days Bob's mother arrived at the babysitters before six o'clock, but soon a day came when she arrived after six. Bob was fine. He told his mother it was okay that she came after six because it was just a plan.

Bob's problem with a Mislearned Word was a little different than Charles' problem. Charles simply did not know that a "boink" was the same thing as a "hit." It was fairly easy to tell what the problem was because Charles was telling his mother why his teacher was wrong to suspend him.

The word Bob mislearned was the word promise. He believed that a statement that something was going to happen was a promise and that a promise could not be broken. It is harder to spot these types of Mislearned Words. The clue in this case was that

Bob helpfully kept repeating, "You promised, you promised." It might have been harder to figure out if he had not done this.

Bob had no more tantrums when his mother was "late" picking him up at the babysitters. He understood the difference between a plan and a promise and, while he was still sad when his mother came after six, he no longer felt she had broken a promise and he did not tantrum.

▶ SOCIAL MEANINGS

We are so used to the Social Meanings of words that we often do not realize how complex they can be. Since we learn Social Meanings instinctively, it is difficult for us to identify when our children have not learned these words correctly.

Answering to Your Name

A very common problem is when children fail to respond when we call their names. Before discussing how to correct this problem, there are two other things to consider.

- **If your children answer sometimes, but not other times, investigate whether there could be an auditory processing problem. Try to notice if they fail to respond only in noisy environments. If your children cannot understand what you are saying, they can't respond.**
- **Attention problems can also have the same effect as auditory processing problems. Practice this skill when your children are not involved in a preferred activity.**

In some cases it is simply because your children don't know that the person saying their name wants them to answer.

Carl's Response

Most of the time Carl was very verbal, but, when his mother called his name, he did not respond. Mom knew Carl heard her and assumed his failure to respond was simply part of his autism.

I talked to Carl's mother about teaching him to answer when she called his name. She selected "Yes?" as the Replacement Behavior, to take the place of not responding. "What do you say?" was the Reminder. To motivate Carl, his mother developed a Reward Chart.

After dinner on Friday, Carl's mother explained when someone says Carl's name he should answer by saying "Yes?" They talked about why someone says another person's name and why they would want the other person to answer - even if they have not asked a question. She reminds Carl that when he calls her, she always answers him in some way. She tells him he should say "Yes?" when he hears his name.

Carl's mother role played with Carl. First Carl said her name and she answered "Yes," then she said his name and waited for his answer. They did this several times. Mom told Carl if he forgot she would remind him by saying, "What do you say?"

Carl's mother showed him the Reward Chart and told him he would get two points if he answered by himself or if he answered with one Reminder. If he needed more than one Reminder, he'd still get one point when he answered.

After the lesson was over, Carl's mother waited until Carl's favorite TV show was over. Then she called, "Carl." When he didn't answer, she said, "What do you say?" and Carl answered, "Yes."

Carl's mother repeated the lesson twice a day over the weekend and every day for a week. She made sure to call his name frequently, but to avoid times that he was intensely engaged in his special interests. She gave him a lot of praise and showed him his points on his Reward Chart.

Although Carl needed a lot of Reminders at first, he got better at answering on his own. After a while, Carl developed the habit of answering when he heard his name and no longer needed the Reward Chart.

The most important part of this lesson was for Carl to learn that a response was expected when his name was called. It was very important to make sure Carl was rewarded when he got this right, even if a lot of prompting was required.

I have used this method many times over the years and it is often successful. Just like with neurotypical children, however, there will be times your children will not answer. But, that is normal. The idea is to have your ASD children understand that hearing their name indicates that the person saying it wants a response.

Rude Comments

Children with ASD often get in trouble when they try to copy the behavior of other children at school. Not only do they not know how to conceal their behavior, but they do not understand the Social Signals that students send each other indicating their acceptance of rude behavior.

> *Philip's Racial Slurs*
> *Some of the boys at Philip's middle school are into Gangster Rap. Philip wants to be part of their group and tries to act like them. Philip was called to the principal's office for using the N word to another student.*

Philip does not understand that words he says can be hurtful and wrong. While he does become upset if he is called names, he doesn't understand that other students can also become upset. Since the popular kids use these words, he feels he could be popular if he does the same.

While a simple list of prohibited words should be all that is needed to correct this type of problem, it often is not. In some cases, your children will persist in these behaviors because they are convinced that it is cool. In other cases, the use of these words has become a habit or tic and stopping the behavior has some involuntary components.

In addition, by the time your children reach middle school, they are often convinced of the cluelessness of adults. When your children are younger, it is a good idea to include information about rude and hurtful words in your Everyday Learning lessons.

When adults try to explain to children with ASD not to say hurtful things, they may use words that have Social Meanings that your children simply don't understand.

> *Kenny's Comments*
> *Kenny is a very bright high school student who is vocal in his opinions. He has commented on a security guard's gold teeth and discussed his own private parts in school. He has even told fellow students that their religion is wrong because it disagrees with his religion.*

Kenny does not understand that what he says is inappropriate. He does not know how to take the perspective of another person and express his opinions in a socially acceptable manner.

Kenny's school suggested using the following paragraph to help him learn to be more appropriate.

> **Sometimes I say things which can hurt or insult others' feelings. I sometimes need to express my feelings and thoughts and that is OK. I will express these feelings and thoughts with a "safe person." Using put-down or demeaning language is not OK.**

When Kenny is asked if he understands this paragraph he says he does; but does he really? Let's take a look at this paragraph and see if it will work for Kenny.

- **Sometimes I say things which can hurt or insult others' feelings.**

    This can work if we give Kenny a clear definition of what it means to hurt or insult. He can be taught what these words mean, even though he might confuse the word hurt with physical pain and this will make it harder for him to learn the lesson. He knows people have feelings and can learn that sometimes when he says things they can have this effect.

- **I sometimes need to express my feelings and thoughts and that is OK.**

Kenny has feelings and thoughts and he is very able to express these thoughts, so this sentence is fine.

- **I will express these feelings and thoughts with a "safe person."**

Now we are starting to run into trouble. Exactly which feelings and thoughts will Kenny want to discuss with his safe person? Since he has feelings and thoughts throughout the day, how can he determine which ones to discuss? While it is fine to encourage Kenny to discuss any matter with his safe person, this doesn't help him with the hurtful and inappropriate things he might say. Kenny's problem is that he can't judge what is, and what is not, hurtful or insulting.

- **Using put-down or demeaning language is not OK.**

Now we are in real trouble. The words put-down and demeaning are Social Words. They have very complex Social Meanings. Not only has he no standard by which to judge which statements hurt or insult, but he has no Theory of Mind to decide when someone would feel something he says is a put-down or demeaning.

When Kenny fails to understand that a comment about another student's religion could be considered a put-down, he gets into serious trouble at school.

There is another way to help Kenny learn to judge what statements he can make. He needs to learn the specific content to avoid. The following paragraph and list helped to solve the problem.

> **Sometimes I say things which can insult others' feelings. Even if I state a fact, it can make someone feel this way. If I want to state a fact or give an opinion about the subjects on my list, I can write it down or remember it. I can ask one of my safe persons if it is okay before I say it to someone else.**

Let's take a look at this paragraph and see if it will work for Kenny.

- **Sometimes I say things which can insult others' feelings.**

   This will work better because "insult" has a clear definition. Kenny understands words using their dictionary meanings. He knows people have feelings.

- **Even if I state a fact, it can make someone feel this way.**

   As with Tina who told a classmate she smelled bad, Kenny doesn't always understand which facts can be hurtful. He needs to learn this one fact at a time.

- **If I want to state a fact or give an opinion about the subjects on my list, I can write it down or remember it.**

Kenny has a list that tells him exactly which subjects he must treat with caution. He does not have to guess which thoughts and feelings are a problem. He also knows that subjects that are not on his list are okay to talk about.

- **I can ask one of my safe persons if it is okay before I say it to someone else.**

Now Kenny knows that his feelings and thoughts about the subjects on his list are okay to talk about in the right setting. It also gives his safe persons an opportunity to help him understand why certain comments are, or are not, appropriate.

Developing a list for Kenny was challenging. Because he is so bright and has such an inquiring mind, he has many areas of interest. Working with his family, we came up with the following list:

> Race
> Ethnicity
> Religion
> Sex
> Politics
> Body Odors
> Private Parts
> Physical Appearance

All this information is presented to Kenny as part of his Everyday Learning. He is attempting to comply, although he frequently forgets. If Kenny finds other inappropriate subjects to discuss, those subjects can be added to his list.[22]

---

22 See Tools to Change Behavior.

SOCIAL SIGNALS

Errors in Social Signals can be the most difficult to correct. Some Signals are actually instincts, while others have been learned instinctively.

Sometimes children with ASD display Signals that are different, neither instincts nor the product of instinctive learning. Displaying the wrong facial expressions or mannerisms may set them apart from their neurotypical peers.

Some children with ASD become excellent performers. I knew one young man who had won an award as the best actor at a local children's theatre two years in a row. He was able to act out appropriate Signals, but he could not apply them outside the performance setting.

▶ SENDING SOCIAL SIGNALS

It is possible to learn some Social Signals through Everyday Learning lessons. The following two examples demonstrate how an individual with ASD can learn appropriate Social Signals.

> *Simon at a Funeral*
> *Occasionally Simon and his wife, Frieda, would have to attend a funeral. Frieda dreaded when this happened. Simon's behavior was highly inappropriate - he had strange facial expressions and*

made odd remarks. On some occasions he would giggle.

Frieda taught Simon to make a slightly sad or neutral face by practicing with a mirror. She also taught him three or four appropriate phrases to use, such as, "I'm sorry for your loss," and cautioned him not to use any other words. She told him it was not appropriate to giggle.

The next time they went to a funeral Simon followed Frieda's instructions and his behavior at the funeral was appropriate.

Simon's wife had been unable to teach him how to select his own appropriate Signals, but he was capable of learning and using Signals she taught him. With her success at teaching Simon appropriate behavior for funerals, Frieda decided to tackle his behavior at dinner parties.

Simon at a Dinner Party

Simon didn't understand dinner parties were opportunities to socialize. He thought he was only there to eat. When someone asked him a question, he would answer quickly and immediately return to his meal.

Frieda told Simon that when they were dining with friends he was supposed to engage in brief conversations during the meal. She told him if he was asked a question, he had to have a short conversation exchanging at least three or four statements back and forth before beginning to eat again.

Simon followed these instructions and his behavior dining out was more appropriate.

In the example of the dinner party, the Signal Simon was sending was that he was disinterested in the other people at the table.

This wasn't the case. He enjoyed their company but didn't know how to interact over dinner. Once he was given a clear set of instructions, he was able to participate appropriately and enjoyed the interaction.

Simon's wife was using Everyday Learning to teach him the behaviors that would make him successful at a funeral or at a dinner party.

▶ SELF-TALK

When children talk out loud at inappropriate times, other children frequently reject them. Adults may become angry and want to give them consequences. Children with ASD can get in trouble if they speak out loud to themselves or say the wrong things out loud.

The words used for self-talk are different from Social Words. Social Words are a problem because of the meanings of the Words. Self-talk is a problem because of the reactions of individuals observing the behavior, regardless of the content of the speech. That's what turns these words into Social Signals.

It is difficult for teachers to discuss self-talk because they view it as part of your children's disabilities. When teachers cannot explain why classmates reject ASD children, I always ask if the children make noises or talk to themselves. It is not unusual to receive an affirmative response.

Many ASD children can learn to just think their thoughts without talking instead of saying them out loud. First they need to be made aware that they can think without talking and then they need to practice. Thinking without talking is the Replacement Behavior. In many cases, ASD children simply do not know that they should not be saying their thoughts out loud.

If talking out loud is not just a result of not knowing, but is providing some benefit, changing the behavior requires correcting the underlying problem. This is usually the case with scripting, which is not the same as self-talk. Scripting is when children repeat scripts from TV shows and other types of media. This is often done softly, under their breath, and it serves a different function than simply saying thoughts out loud.

Neurological issues may include verbal tics or making other sounds that are involuntary. This behavior typically does not resolve unless a child's anxiety or other medical issues are treated. If the words are the result of a neurological problem, medical intervention may be required.

Redirecting some ASD children who simply do not know that they shouldn't talk or make sounds out loud can be relatively quick, while other ASD children may have a very, very difficult time.

Adrian's Self-Talk

Adrian was an excellent student in fifth grade. He enjoyed following directions and doing his work. He was never considered a behavior problem, but he frequently talked to himself out loud. While the teachers liked him, they found the self-talk distracting. At home Adrian also talked to himself out loud.

Adrian's self-talk had developed into a habit. No one had ever tried to help him stop talking to himself out loud because they assumed it was part of his disability. Adrian's mother decided that over Christmas Break she would teach him that he should only talk to himself out loud in his room.

She selected the Replacement Behavior to think his thoughts in his head without talking. Adrian's Reminder would be when she put her finger over her lips. She discussed her plan with his teachers and they agreed to help when Adrian returned to school if his mother felt he was ready.

The first day of Christmas Break, mom explained to Adrian that now that he was getting older, he needed to learn more adult rules. She told him that it was alright to talk to himself out loud in his room, but not where other people could see or hear him.

Adrian was curious why his mother would want him to do this. She explained that at his age it is not considered appropriate to talk to yourself out loud - in school it distracted the other children and some people found it annoying. Because Adrian would be going to middle school, she wanted him to make a good impression on his new classmates.

Some people may not want to tell their ASD children that others might think their behavior is annoying. It is my feeling that this is important social information. The decision, however, is up to each individual family.

His mother showed him a Reward Chart that divided his day into 30 minute intervals. She told him he could earn points if he did not talk to himself out loud outside his room or if he stopped talking to himself when she put her finger over her lips. She demonstrated the Reminder. She wanted to know how Adrian felt. Adrian felt that he could remember just to think his thoughts without talking.

The next day, Adrian forgot many times. But, when his mother gave him the Reminder, he stopped. Adrian was able to earn points throughout the day. For the first few days Adrian forgot very frequently. Sometimes he would catch himself and put his own finger over his lips. Sometimes he would go to his room and talk to himself out loud. He still got his points if he did this.

By the end of Christmas Break, Adrian was greatly improved, even though when he was distracted or stressed he would forget. When he went back to school, his mother brought his Reward Chart for him to use at school and showed the teachers his Reminder.

Adrian greatly reduced the amount of time he was talking to himself out loud in school. His teachers used the Reward Chart and his Reminder and were extremely happy with his progress. The other children seemed more comfortable with Adrian. After several months, he had stopped talking out loud at school almost all the time and rarely talked out loud at home except in his room.

Martin's Sounds
Martin is an anxious, tense child. He becomes stressed very easily. In his second grade class, he has no friends. Martin talks to himself almost all the time.

When Martin's mother first talked to him about talking in his head without saying words out loud, he became very tense and upset. His mother waited until the next day to try to talk to him again; this time he also became upset.

The following day his mother told Martin he could have his favorite snack right after they practiced thinking his thoughts in his head without talking out loud. This time, focused on a reward, Martin practiced for three, one minute intervals.

Then Martin's mother introduced a Reward Chart. She told him that while he was at home, sometimes they would practice thinking without talking. She told him that she would schedule a half hour each night, and reward him for every five minutes he said no words out loud unless he was talking to another family member or was alone in his room. She showed him that she would set a timer so they would know how much time passed.

The first time she started the five minute session with a timer Martin did not talk for the whole five minutes. Martin, however, was unable to keep from talking out loud during the second five minute interval. After two minutes he began talking and his mother immediately reset the timer for five minutes to give him another chance. This time Martin was only able to keep from talking for one minute.

Martin's mother revised the plan to try five, three minute intervals - a total of 15 minutes. The next day, Martin's mother told him about the change and asked him if he was ready to try again. He was to get his favorite snack after the practice session whether or not he got any points.

Martin's progress was very slow. His mother slowly extended the time during which he would think in his head without talking. Unless he was sick or very tired, he was eventually able to go without talking out loud for an entire half hour.

While Martin made very slow progress, the lessons were building a foundation for the future. Martin had learned a new skill and might at a later time become better able to use it.

When your children are very young, you can tell them to think without talking and remind them to do this simply as part of Everyday Learning. But, once this habit is established, it can be very difficult for some children to stop.

▶ OTHER WORDS

Roy's remarks are different from self-talk. He is commenting on the behavior of others, not talking to himself. His words are inappropriate because he is sending a Signal that he disrespects his classmates and teachers.

It is true that Roy believes their mistakes are stupid - in fact we all occasionally think rude thoughts about others. It is not necessary to change what Roy is thinking; it is necessary for him to learn not to say these thoughts out loud.

> *Roy's Reminder*
> *Roy made loud, rude remarks when other students or teachers made mistakes. His plan was to either silently write down his comments or think them in his head without talking.*

Roy was in a gifted class in middle school. He had no friends. Even among his gifted peers, Roy's intelligence stood out. With an IQ of 149, he rarely had to study and almost never made a mistake in academic pursuits. His social issues, on the other hand, were significant. When students in his class or a teacher made a mistake, he would make rude or critical remarks out loud. Despite repeated lectures and punishments, Roy continued to make these remarks.

Roy was asked to work with his autism support teacher to change this habit. As an incentive, he could earn points during any class period in which he did not make a rude remark and would select a reward at home. His teachers would mark his points on his Reward Chart.

The autism teacher and Roy met a number of times and reviewed past incidents. Roy completely understood which remarks were offensive and understood the goal to think his thoughts without talking. He felt it would be really hard for him to remember not to make these remarks. When the autism teacher suggested he could write his comments down, he felt it would be easier than just not saying anything.

Roy's autism teacher showed him a written plan and they worked together to put it into Roy's own words. He agreed not to show his notes to other students, but to share them with his safe persons. Roy's mother agreed to review his Reward Chart and provide rewards at home.

Roy was given a laminated version of his plan and was instructed to put it in his notebook where he could see it during class. His teachers agreed to walk by his desk and tap the laminated copy if Roy forgot what to do.

Roy had no trouble understanding that his remarks were rude and that they made his classmates angry. He simply felt a strong need to express these types of thoughts. He needed a Replacement Behavior to help him stop; the Replacement Behavior needed to be appropriate in school. Writing down the comments gave Roy a way to express what he was thinking without disrupting the class.

It is often easier for ASD children to write down inappropriate vocalizations than to try to stop making them without this interim step. The writing down is closer to the vocalizations than simply thinking them without talking.

Before being able to institute this plan, Roy's counselor had to consult with his teachers. When Roy decided he wanted to write down his thoughts, it was understood that he might be putting some very inappropriate comments on paper. His teachers agreed he would only be required to show these notes to the counselor, the autism support teacher, and his mother.

At first, Roy would forget to put his Reminder on his desk and without it there he would make comments. His teachers would remind him to put it on his desk. With the card on his desk, he remembered most of the time and received points.

At first, he wrote down a lot of comments. As time went on, however, he became better at just thinking the comments and, when he felt ready, he put his Reminder away.

▶ OTHER HABITS THAT SEND SOCIAL SIGNALS

Certain habits can send terrible Social Signals. Once habits are formed, they can be extremely difficult to break.

> *Frank's Nose Picking*
> *Twelve year old Frank is bright, does well academically, and has relatively good social skills, but, Frank does not have any friends. Throughout the day, Frank picks his nose.*

> To help Frank break this habit required an intense effort. The effort began with the beginning of the summer break, because attempts during the school year had been unsuccessful. Frank's parents adopted a structured reward system with highly desirable rewards.

Initially, they encouraged Frank not to pick his nose for a half hour a night. If he was not able to do that, he could choose to use a tissue or to go to the bathroom to pick his nose, and still earn his points. Frank was able to do this and earned points toward a reward. And, as they extended the time, Frank frequently used the tissue and refrained from picking his nose outside of the bathroom.

After practicing for the entire summer, Frank had mastered using a tissue and had stopped picking his nose in public.

Frank's parents had tried periodically to help Frank stop picking his nose in public, but unfortunately, by the age of twelve, this was a very difficult habit to break. If you have young children who do this, it is important to redirect them before a habit is formed.

▶ UNDERSTANDING SOCIAL SIGNALS

Understanding Social Signals is in many ways the most difficult part for children with ASD. It is a more difficult problem than trying to teach your children to use the right Social Signals. Failing to have an instinctive understanding of Signals leaves children with ASD at an extreme disadvantage.

While we can start to teach some of these Signals, it is often best to try to figure out ways to alleviate our children's issues and concerns in other ways. It is fairly common that children with ASD run into problems with Social Signals at school.

You will remember Cindy who thought her teacher was yelling at her each time the teacher reprimanded other students in her class.

Cindy's Upset

Cindy sometimes came home very upset because she was in trouble at school; she would cry herself to sleep. Cindy said she was in trouble because the teacher yelled at her.

Before being able to help Cindy, we needed the cooperation of her teacher. It was agreed if the teacher ever needed to correct Cindy, she would stand directly in front of Cindy and say, "I need to talk to you about a problem." We did not choose a phrase using Cindy's name because then just hearing her name might trigger fear.

After talking to her teacher, Cindy's mother spoke with her. She explained if the teacher wanted to tell her about a problem she would say, "I need to talk to you about a problem," while standing directly in front of her. If her teacher didn't say this when she was standing in front of her, then the teacher was not talking to her about a problem.

Cindy's mother also explained that sometimes the teacher had to correct other children in the class, but she did not always use their names. She explained that sometimes the teacher sounded angry when she talked to other students, but that did not mean she was angry with Cindy.

Cindy and her mother role played. First Cindy's mother would say "stop talking" while looking away from Cindy and standing far away; then she would say "stop talking" looking just above Cindy standing a little way away. She would say "stop talking" in a loud mean voice. Then she would have Cindy say "stop talking," looking and standing away from her mother and again looking over her mother's head. She encouraged Cindy to try to "sound angry."

They talked about why the teacher wanted the other students to stop talking and how talking loudly disrupted the class. They also practiced talking loudly and talking softly, so Cindy could get an idea of the difference. They talked about other things that could disrupt the class - like throwing papers.

This interaction was repeated before Cindy went to bed on Friday, twice on Saturday, and again twice on Sunday. By the time Monday morning rolled around, Cindy seemed to understand. When Cindy got to school Monday morning, her mother went with her to class early and asked Cindy's teacher to repeat the lesson with Cindy.

Cindy could not read Social Signals and thought any comment to the class was directed at her. This is actually a very common problem.

When teachers are correcting their class, they frequently use eye contact and do not use names. Many children with ASD become fearful of school because when a teacher yells at other students your children may think they are yelling at them.

Because Cindy has a great deal of difficulty recognizing Social Signals, this lesson was very difficult for her. Her mother and teacher continued practicing with Cindy for some time. Because Cindy may never be able to distinguish these types of Social Signals, it was necessary to create a system she could learn quickly.

As time passed, Cindy's anxiety was reduced and she felt more comfortable in class. Cindy no longer came home from school upset. Crafting these individual rules can be tricky, but they really can change a negative situation into a positive one.

If your children are afraid to go to school, if they cry and show fear before school, consider this a possibility. These situations happen with some frequency and often your children's teachers insist your children are fine and cannot understand your concerns.

SOCIAL SETTING

Social Setting includes where you are and who you are with. When you are with your family, you behave differently than when you are at work; when you are at the beach, you behave differently than when you are at a play. When you are in different settings, you have different reactions. And, while I am saying something that is very obvious to you, these differences may not be obvious to your children.

All children are routinely taught the behavior to follow in certain Social Settings. You would tell your children ahead of time exactly what to expect and what to do at a wedding or a funeral. But, in most cases, we don't explain these differences.

In many cases, the correct use of Social Actions and Words depend on the Social Setting. Whenever possible, it is best to teach the correct Social Action for a given situation. Many serious problems occur because ASD children do not recognize which Words and Actions are acceptable in different settings. As you learn more about Social Settings, you will be able to help your children be more successful.

When teachers speak to you about problems your children have encountered, you may want to ask about the Social Settings in which the problems occurred. It is not unusual that problems are specific to certain settings.

▶ WHERE YOU ARE

Many behaviors are only acceptable in certain Social Settings. When a behavior that is acceptable in one Setting is used in another Setting, serious problems can arise.

Bathroom Rules

When family rules allow or even require their children to leave the bathroom door open, ASD children have to be taught there are different rules outside the home. Especially because parents assist young children with toileting when they are in public bathrooms, ASD children may not realize the rules are different.

Timmy does not know that the rules for going to the bathroom are different at home and at school. No one taught him that at school he had to close the bathroom door and have his pants up when he left the bathroom. When his teachers yelled at him, he became frightened and confused, unable to process this confusing and complicated information.

> **Timmy's Toileting**
> **Timmy's kindergarten teacher called his parents for a conference. Timmy refused to close the door when he went to the bathroom; he would walk out of the bathroom with his pants down.**
>
> Timmy's parents decided it would confuse him to have different bathroom rules at home and at school. They decided to change the rules at home. All family members would close the door when they used the bathroom and leave the bathroom with their pants up.
> Timmy's Behavior Lessons began after school on a Friday, after the new rules were explained to him and to his brother. Timmy's mom took pictures

of Timmy inside the bathroom with the door closed and put the picture on a poster on the back of the door.

She talked to Timmy about how some things are private and that private means you do something by yourself where no one else can see you. She told him that he knows no one else can see him in the bathroom because the door is closed and no one else is in the room. She asked Timmy to think of other times that no one could see him.

She explained his mother, father, and grandmother can help him in the bathroom at home because they are part of his family and gave him a paper with their pictures and a picture of a toilet. She listened to what Timmy had to say about this new rule and she answered his questions.

Over the weekend, Timmy's mom paid close attention to Timmy. When she believed he needed to go, she reminded him of the new rules. She made a Reward Chart with ten boxes and told him he could get a Thomas the Train sticker each time he followed the new bathroom rules. She told him when all the boxes were filled, he would get a special Thomas the Train reward.

Timmy's parents also spoke with his teacher. They suggested the school use a daily Reward Chart and give Timmy a sticker in the morning and in the afternoon when he used the bathroom properly. They asked to get a copy of the Reward Chart each week, so they could reward Timmy at home for doing a good job at school.

Every day his mother told him what a good job he was doing. If he made a mistake, she told him not to worry, that he was learning something new and it would take time. Over several weeks, Timmy was doing much better.

In addition to new learning, Timmy had to break an old habit. It was easy for him to forget to close the door or pull up his pants. Eventually, however, the new habit took hold.

At school, Timmy's teacher and principal did not believe that his problem had anything to do with learning a new skill. While the teacher accepted his checklist and stickers, she made no comment to his mother. The checklist and stickers were put on the teacher's desk and never used.

However, when the teacher yelled at Timmy to close the bathroom door, he no longer refused. And, when he would forget at school and leave the bathroom without his clothes, he no longer had a tantrum when his teacher told him to put his clothes on. The teacher's reprimands simply acted as Reminders because Timmy knew what to do. Eventually, Timmy learned to use his new skills consistently at school.

Privacy is a complex social concept. It is a good idea to talk about privacy when your children are young so they can build an understanding as they get older. And, while "not being able to see other people" can be taught to most children with ASD, understanding whether or not other people can see them may be much more difficult.

For boys the problem is more complicated than for girls. They need to learn the rules for using urinals as soon as possible. This requires a male member of the family or male friend to actually teach the social norms of male bathroom behavior. For example, when there are several urinals, you should select one that is not next to another person unless no other urinal is available. Teaching this doesn't mean showing your boys what to do just once, but many times until they understand where to stand, where to look, and all the related concepts of using a urinal.

It is important for our children to both understand the Social Sense of what is private and to learn the Social Actions that keep their behavior private.

▶ WHO IS PRESENT

Who is present is also extremely important. Many individuals with ASD have difficulty in the workplace because they do not understand Social Setting issues. Correcting your boss isn't so bad if you are in private; it is really bad if you correct your boss in front of his boss!

For the most part, your children can get into a whole lot more trouble by saying the wrong thing, in the wrong place, at the wrong time, than by waiting for the right time – a private conversation.

> *Daniel's Movie Date*
> *Daniel was in eighth grade and had no friends, but he was getting along great with Mike. In their Tae Kwon Do class they would work on routines and joke around. Daniel wanted to see if Mike would go to the new Chuck Norris movie with him.*
> *As Mike talked to his girlfriend, Daniel walked over. He asked Mike for his phone number so he could call him to go to a movie. Mike turned away from Daniel and avoided him from then on.*

Misreading a Social Setting can sometimes be disastrous. Mike's rejection of Daniel - because this question was asked in front of Mike's girlfriend - was devastating. To help Daniel learn how to avoid this type of rejection in the future, it is important to give him some Social Setting guidelines.

You may want to teach your children that when they want to make plans with someone, or they want to talk about a problem they have with someone, it is best to talk to that person when they are alone. Following this rule would have stopped Daniel from talking about some safe subjects, like a ride to school, but for the most part it should serve him well.

Learning about Social Settings is very important for other reasons. Karen's cuddling created a very uncomfortable and possibly unsafe situation. Unless Karen knew when it was okay to "cuddle" she could have very serious problems.

> **Karen's Cuddles**
> **Ten year old Karen cuddles with her dad and sits on his lap. She may put her hand on his stomach or his thigh as she wiggles around. When Uncle Harold visited from out of town, to his embarrassment, Karen sat herself down on his lap and began to "cuddle."**

Karen's mother felt Karen could understand there are different rules for what she could do with different people. If she didn't think Karen could understand this, then she would have had to completely prohibit the behavior.

She made Karen a list of the family members with whom she could cuddle - her mother, her father, and her maternal grandmother. When Karen was calm and relaxed, mom and dad sat with her and talked about cuddling. They explained they were happy when Karen cuddled with them and asked her what she thought about cuddling.

They took turns having Karen sit on their laps and showed her how she would touch their thigh or stomach without realizing where her hands were. They let her know that that was okay until now, but now that she was getting older she should not touch anyone on the stomach or thigh.

They showed her the list with pictures, and told her she could cuddle only with the people on her list. If anyone else wanted to "cuddle," Karen had to ask her parents first.

The lesson was repeated two more times over the weekend, until Karen's parents felt sure she understood. Because this behavior was so serious, they repeated the lesson once a week for several weeks, showing Karen the list with the pictures.

It is obvious to us that Karen's behavior is inappropriate with her uncle and it is important to help Karen understand the error she made so she can be safe in the future. Karen simply didn't know that this cuddling behavior should be restricted to interactions with very close family members. She does not have the social judgment to make this decision herself.

Because this lesson is so important, Karen's parents went to great lengths to be sure she understood what to do. They could, of course, have simply told Karen not to cuddle anymore with anyone, but then she would not have learned the difference between different levels of intimacy, an important component of Social Sense.

▶ WHERE YOU ARE AND WHO YOU ARE WITH

Many issues combine two aspects of Social Setting problems – both where you are and who you are with. This is what happened to William when he got in trouble at school.

It is very common for children with ASD to make errors related to personal space. They often get in trouble because they do not understand the appropriate distances to keep between people and the parts of the body they are allowed to touch. The parts of the body that can be touched are different with family members and individuals outside the family.

William Gets Jill's Attention
William and Jill sit next to each other in school. They are good friends. One day, Jill was looking down at her work and William touched her face to get her to look up. Jill got upset and William got in trouble with his teacher.

William's parents sat down with him after dinner when he was not distracted and was relaxed. They explained to him that there are rules about where and how you can touch other people and that the rules were different for family members and other people. This Social Sense information is very important for William.

William was surprised because in his family touching someone's face was never a problem, but he said he understood the rule. His parents gave him a list of the family members he could touch on the face and told him not to touch anyone else on the face. The list included his parents, grandparents, his brother, his aunts and uncles, and his cousins.

Then his parents helped him role play the right way to get someone's attention. They had him show them how Jill was sitting and role played tapping her on the top of her shoulder or on the outside of her arm.

Poor William was very confused; he really hadn't done anything wrong. He had not hurt Jill. Even so, just because he touched her face, he was in trouble. Had William done this at home, it is unlikely there would have been a problem. When William's parents tried to explain William's problem to his teacher, she refused to change his punishment and refused to believe he didn't know what he did was wrong.

When you are teaching a rule, remember not to prohibit behaviors that regularly occur in your children's daily lives unless you are willing to make everyone change their behavior. While some families might not regularly touch each other on the face, William's family does.

After providing this Everyday Learning lesson to William, his parents explained there are other things you can do with family members that you can't do with other people. They talked about other things that are only allowed with family.

How and where you can touch another person not only varies from culture to culture, but also from family to family. William simply needed to learn this new rule. It was not hard for him to understand. Had the problem continued after this incident, or if touching others had been an ongoing problem in his class, a different approach would have been required.

For children with ASD it is best to set very conservative guidelines. No one will be too offended if you touch them only in the "right" places, or not at all.

Like William, Brett was in serious trouble because of his failing to understand his Social Setting.

Brett's School Behavior
In kindergarten, Brett is aggressive with other children and calls them names. At home, he is very loving, but interacts aggressively with his six-foot-tall, fourteen year old brother, Samuel.

Brett was suspended after he hit a classmate very hard in the face.

Brett was suspended on a Thursday, for one day. By coincidence, the following Monday was a teachers' work day, so there were four days to prepare Brett to return to school.

In talking with Brett's mother, I learned that he plays very aggressively with his brother. In fact, since six year old Brett doesn't have any playmates his age, he spends most of his play time with older children.

Brett adores his brother, but sometimes annoys him. They can be very rough with each other. When Brett hits his brother, he hits him very hard - as hard as he can hit. His brother barely notices. Since neither one gets hurt, this interaction is tolerated at home.

In addition, Brett hears his cousins calling names and using rude expressions, such as making an "L" on their foreheads and calling "loser, loser." Once again, this behavior has not been formally corrected at home, although Brett's mother and father frequently tell the children to stop.

Brett's parents must quickly change his behavior, but his brother Samuel also has ASD. Changing behavior at home will take a long time, so they decide instead to simply teach Brett what behaviors to use at school. They ask Brett's teacher if it would be all right for him to walk up to her without raising his hand if he is upset. Brett's teacher agrees this would be okay.

Even though Brett can't read, they write out Brett's plan so they don't forget any of the things they need to review with him. They choose "grabbing his shirt" as the Replacement Behavior for hitting and saying, "I am angry," as the Replacement Behavior for inappropriate words.

The plan uses the words that Brett uses for things he does at home that are not allowed at school. They hope if they read it with him many times, he will remember it in the same way he remembers many of the stories they read together.

Brett's parents arranged a variety of activities for Samuel over the weekend. They did not feel that Brett would be able to concentrate while his brother was home. His mother wanted to work calmly with Brett, with as little interruption as possible.

On Friday morning, after his brother went to school, Brett's mother sat down to talk with him. She tells him she is going to explain to him why he got in trouble at school. She reminds him that when he hits Samuel, Samuel doesn't cry. She asks why he thinks the child at school was crying. Brett is unable to think of a reason.

Mom explains that Samuel is very big and if Brett hits him it does not hurt him at all or sometimes just a little. She tells Brett if he hits children who are smaller than Samuel, it hurts them. Because he hurt Lucas, Lucas was crying. She explains if he hit mom, it would hurt her. She tells Brett he is not supposed to hit any children who are smaller than Samuel.

Mom and Brett talk about what it feels like to get hit and why people don't like to be hit. Then she talks to him about the games he likes to play at home, like "wrestling holds." She explains that even though he can play these games with Samuel, these games can hurt children who are smaller than Samuel. She takes out the plan she developed and reads it to Brett.

Plan for Brett

There are things you do at home you cannot do at school. It is very important not to do these things at school.

Any kind of "playing around" is not allowed at school.

> **No acting like a Power Ranger**
> **No Tae Kwon Do**
> **No biting or scratching**
> **No hitting or punching**
> **No choking or hugging (wrestling holds)**

If someone makes you angry or you want to do any of the things on this list, take your hands and grab your shirt. Then walk up to your teacher and tell her what is wrong.

Certain words are not allowed at school. Do not say:

> **Jerk**
> **Loser**
> **Double Loser**
> **Stupid**
> **I'm going to kick your butt**

If someone makes you angry and you want to say one of these things, say "I am angry." Then walk over to your teacher and tell her what is wrong.

They talk about what Brett can do when he gets angry. Brett said he can say, "I am angry," but he does not want to grab his shirt. He says he could hold his hands together behind his back. He told his mom that he could do some deep breathing when he gets angry. Mom lets Brett know that he has good ideas and that they will change the plan so he can do those things.

Brett says he can walk to the teacher if he is angry and asks a lot of questions about what games and words are allowed at school.

Mom tells Brett that he may see other children at school do some of the things on his list. She explains they are "playing around" and they are breaking the rules at school. She tells him it is not okay for him to break the rules, even if other children break them. She lets Brett know he can follow the rules.

Mom also explains Brett might hear other children at school say some of the words on his list. She explains they are saying words that are not allowed at school and just because they are breaking the rules, it does not mean that it is okay for him to break the rules. She lets Brett know he can follow the rules.

Mom role plays with Brett. She pretends that she is angry with another child in her class and says, "I am angry," then she puts her hands behind her back and walks to the teacher. Then Brett pretends that he is angry at another child and says, "I am angry." He puts his hands behind his back and walks to the teacher. He also practices taking deep breaths.

Mom went over this lesson at least three times a day over the long weekend and Brett was fully engaged and interested each time. His mom also went over the lesson right before going to school on Tuesday and reminded Brett's teacher that he would walk up to her if he was having a problem.

You noticed in this plan, Brett was able to make a suggestion on how the plan was implemented. He did not want to "grab his shirt," but he was comfortable with putting his hands behind his back and he wanted to do deep breathing. It is very important to incorporate your children's ideas in their plans if those ideas are appropriate.

As often happens in these situations, the change in Brett's behavior when he returned to school was immediate and dramatic. He followed his plan and did not get in trouble - for ten days.

After ten school days of excellent behavior, Brett's teacher called to say that he again hit another child. When he got home, his mom asked him what happened. Brett said, "I know, I know, I forgot. Deep breathing, deep breathing, hands behind my back. I forgot."

Brett started earning class rewards and was very happy in school. He also decided that the school rules should become house rules and asked his brother and cousins to follow the school rules at home.

This is a classic Social Setting problem. Brett was using the same behaviors at school that he was using at home. When Brett got in trouble for this behavior at school, it never occurred to anyone that he was simply acting the way he did at home. We are so used to changing our behavior to fit our Settings that we don't even think about someone needing to have this explained.

SOCIAL SENSE

Social Sense tells us why we should behave in a certain way. It can be used to try to understand why other people act the way they do. It is the common sense of social interaction.

Your children need to be able to think about the reasons they are engaged in a particular social interaction. The inability to instinctively understand why social interactions happen and some of the "hidden" rules is often the major reason our children have problems in unfamiliar social situations.

Some degree of Social Sense may be taught to your children. By providing information about Social Actions, Words, Signals and Settings, with clearly stated guidelines, we can help our children learn to make better social decisions on their own. Your children can use their observations to try to figure out if a current social interaction matches one they have already learned; or, in a unique situation, they may learn to use certain neutral responses.

As they learn to consider why social events occur, they may begin to use their intellectual abilities to figure out social interactions. Remember my family friend who avoided a fight because he stayed away from the boy with weird hair.

If you think about it, this is similar to the way children learn language, one word at a time.

When I pointed things out when we were in the car, it was just part of a natural conversation; but it was also pointing out how observing behavior gives clues to the reasons people act the way they do. When I asked what the children thought about different people we saw, I was pointing out Social Actions, Words, Signals and Settings. By talking about what we saw and what it might mean, they were learning the reasons someone might act in a certain way. I was teaching Social Sense.

Even more difficult are the different social rules that are unstated. Johnny's difficulty in the Hot Potato game was a result of his difficulty with Social Sense. Even though he heard the rules, he did not understand his part in the game. You can't "see" the rule that you are part of a game. You can't "hear" the rule that you are part of a game. But, to be successful, Johnny had to know that he was part of a game. Someone had to tell him there was a rule that you can't walk away with the ball when you are part of a game.

The difference from neurotypical peers is that you have to specifically identify unstated social rules to help your children. And, while there will be different levels of ability to acquire Social Sense, it never can hurt to point out the reasons things happen.

Social Sense is a matter of analysis and understanding. By observing, we form conclusions about why people are doing and saying certain things. Your children have different levels of ability to form judgments on their own, but any guidance you provide may help them avoid problems in the future.

It is important to try to provide as much information about Social Sense as possible. We have to help our children learn to pay careful attention to their world so they can identify the Social Actions, Words, Signals, and Settings that will give them clues on what they need to do and say. We need to teach as many social rules as possible, so our children can be successful.

▶ UNSTATED RULES

As long as I have been an advocate, I have routinely invited the families I worked with to my house. It was important for me to meet the children in person before attempting to advocate for them. I advocated for children with a wide range of disabilities. It was interesting to see the consistency with which ASD children misunderstood the social rules of visiting. Children who were not in the spectrum, regardless of their disabilities, did not make the same errors.

Wandering

Many of the ASD children who visited my house would simply wander from room to room without seeking permission from me or from their parents. While their parents would try to correct them, they simply looked bewildered and continued to wander or would become upset.

The rule is, "When you are in someone else's home, you need permission to walk around." It is expected for toddlers and even three year olds to make this type of mistake, but by the time children are about four years old they are expected to know that you do not do this. How do they know? The same way the two-year-old learns not to call the lady on the checkout line fat. They learn it instinctively.

But think about how difficult this is. You do not have to ask permission to walk around in your aunt's house or your grandmother's house, not even in your friends' houses. How would you know not to walk around without permission in my house?

This is one of those Social Actions that can be taught ahead of a visit using Everyday Learning. However, once it is an established pattern, a Behavior Lesson may be required to change the behavior. The Replacement Behavior is to stay near your parents until you are given permission to walk around. The Social Sense is that when you are in someone else's home, you need to have permission to walk around. You can create a list of homes where your children have already received permission to walk around without asking.

Opening Doors

While children with ASD wander about, they routinely open closed doors. Other children do not do this. When this happens, their parents are distressed.

The rule is, "When a door is closed in someone else's home, you need permission to open it." Again, how would your children know? They can open any door they want at home or at grandmother's house, why is this house different?

This again is Everyday Learning that can be taught from the time a child is very young. Once a habit is established however, it may require a Behavior Lesson to teach the Replacement Behavior to ask permission before opening a closed door. The Social Sense is that sometimes when doors are closed it is because the person who owns the house doesn't want you to open it, so you need to ask first.

I have noticed that many young ASD children are very interested in bathrooms. If this is a special interest for your children, you may need to walk next to them through a house you are visiting to remind them not to open closed doors until they have permission. If these have been significant or long standing problems, you may want to use a Reward Chart to help your children remember these new rules.

▶ LEARNING TO USE SOCIAL SENSE TO KNOW WHAT TO DO

Sometimes we can teach ASD children to develop their Social Sense by helping them understand better how the world works. As they gain more knowledge about social behaviors, they are better equipped to be successful. It is important to teach the Social Sense of different behavior in different places.

> *Paul's Water*
>
> *When it's time for Paul's class to get water after recess, the teacher tells them, "It's time to go to the water fountain." All the children except Paul line up. Paul walks directly to the water fountain, cutting in front of the line.*

Paul was, of course, responding to the literal words his teacher was saying. She said to go to the water fountain and that is what Paul did. But, how could Paul have used Social Sense to avoid this error? What were his Social Sense errors?

- **Paul did not realize that he was part of a group.**
- **He didn't realize everyone in the group could not get a drink at the same time.**
- **He didn't understand the purpose of lining up.**
- **He didn't realize everyone else in his group followed the instruction using a different Action than he used.**

Paul's mother decides to help Paul develop his Social Sense using this experience and lets his teacher know she is going to work with him over the weekend to learn what to do after recess.

During a quiet time after dinner on Friday, Paul's mother explains that on Monday he will get on line at the water fountain after recess.

Paul did not realize he was part of a group.

She lets Paul know that when many children do things together they are considered a group. She tells him all the students in his third grade class are a group and lets Paul know that he is part of the group. When he is at school, his group is his class.

Paul didn't realize everyone in the group could not get a drink at the same time.

She asks Paul to think about going to the water fountain after recess. She asks him to tell her how many children are in his class and they talk about why only one child at a time can get a drink at the water fountain.

They talk about how Paul is thirsty after recess and how all the other children in his class are probably also thirsty.

Paul didn't understand the purpose of lining up.

Paul's mother asks him if he can think of a way that all the children could get a drink after recess without blocking each other at the water fountain. Paul says the children could get on line and his mother congratulates him on his idea.

They talk about other kinds of groups. Paul loves soccer and baseball. They talk about how each player is a separate person, but how they all work together as a team to win their games. They talk about how when there are many people on a team, they have to take turns. Not all the batters can bat at once, they have to have a "line up" so that they can each take their turn.

Since everyone wants a turn to have water, they talk about how the class has to "line up" to get water. Paul's mother tells him because he is part of his class, he should also get on line with his class to wait for his turn to get water.

They talk about the purpose for a line. Mom reminds Paul about lines at the supermarket and lines at the toy store. She reminds him about the line he walks on at school to go to the cafeteria. She asks him if he can think of other lines he has waited on when there were many people who needed to do the same thing.

Paul didn't realize everyone else in his group followed the instruction using a different Action than he used.

Paul's mother also talked about why he was confused by his teacher's instruction. She told him she knew his teacher would say to "go to the water fountain" when she really meant "go to the line to the water fountain." She asked Paul if he could think of a way he could have figured out his teacher's intended meaning on his own. Again Paul did not know how he could do that.

His mother told him if he watched the other children he would have seen them walk close to the water fountain but then stand on a line. His mother told him that when he is part of a group, he can watch what other members of the group are doing. As long as the other members of the group are doing something he is allowed to do, she suggested Paul could try to do the same Action as others in his group. Paul thought he could do that.

Paul's mother repeated this information and discussed it with Paul on Saturday, Sunday, and Monday morning. They role played several times with his mother saying "go to the water fountain," but with him going to a line instead.

On Monday morning she asked Paul's teacher to walk with him to the line after recess and to praise him if he got on line. Because teachers have many students, it is important to help them remember when your children are learning to do something new.

Paul had no trouble following the new instruction and had a little better understanding of the reason for a line. After his teacher walked Paul to the line for a few days, he was able to get on the line by himself.

▶ LEARNING TO USE SOCIAL SENSE TO KNOW WHAT NOT TO DO

A number of serious problems arise because children with ASD cannot tell when copying peers will get them in trouble. When his mother worked with Paul, she was careful to tell him he could watch the members of his group and do what they are doing ***as long as the other members of the group are doing something he is allowed to do***. This phrase becomes even more important as children get older.

Try as we might, it seems it is not always possible to figure out ***all the rules for things you are not allowed to do***. Once children get older they seem to have a knack for coming up with amazing new ways to do socially inappropriate things.

> **The Bra Snap**
> In Todd's middle school, the boys have a new game. They are "snapping" the girls' bras. Some of the girls think it's funny and Todd wants to be in on the fun. He snaps Sally's bra, but he does it right in front of his teacher.

Once again, a child with ASD gets in serious trouble. Had Todd known that he was not allowed to touch someone's underwear, even through their clothes, there is at least a chance he would not have snapped Sally's bra. But, except for this incident, I doubt anyone would have thought to put this on a list of "things you are not allowed to do."

Over all the years I have been an advocate, I have frequently heard the lament from ASD children that they got in trouble for something everyone else was doing. In most cases, the adults insist that is not the case; no other children have done what this ASD child has done. Charles friends were not boinking and Todd's classmates were not bra snapping. Of course, in each instance, they were.

The Social Sense to conceal a prohibited behavior is frequently, although not always, missing in children with ASD. First, as with Todd and Charles, they may not realize that what they are doing is considered wrong. Second, even if they did, they do not have the skills to know when the teacher can see them.

Other children know how to break the rules without a teacher seeing them; our children don't. They may have heard the expression "doing something behind someone's back," but they do not understand what this means. When they get in trouble for something they see all the other children doing, they think it is unfair.

The expression "behind your back" is not literal, of course. You can be right in front of someone and be doing something "behind their back." And, you can be behind someone, yet doing something of which they are totally aware.

Neither Todd nor Charles could understand why the other boys had not gotten in trouble. The other boys had been careful not to let any adult see what they were doing. Knowing when others are aware of your behavior, or knowing how to stop them from gaining that knowledge, is an important aspect of Social Sense. We can explain to Charles that the other children knew they would get in trouble if an adult saw them boinking so they looked around to see where the adults were before they did it. We can give this same information to Todd about bra snapping.

However, each family will have to decide for themselves whether to actually teach this concept. It is very close to teaching someone to be sneaky; something none of us would want. However, if your children are to relate to typical peers and understand social interactions, it is helpful to understand this. It is difficult to survive, especially in a school environment, without knowing that some behaviors are only for the eyes of peers.

One upside to this whole discussion is that your children may become interested in learning how they can tell whether or not the teacher is looking. This could help them become interested in Social Signals and provide motivation to learn more about them.

▶ LEARNING TO USE SOCIAL SENSE TO UNDERSTAND THE WORLD

Up until now, we have been talking about how ASD children can develop Social Sense to select appropriate behaviors. But, there's another way that our children run into problems with Social Sense. Because they don't really understand how the social world works, they may become more upset than neurotypical peers when things do not happen as planned or when a problem arises.

One common problem is when your children are not picked up at their usual time. They may become frightened and upset, especially if they are unprepared for this.

> *Fred's Tantrum*
>
> *Fred had improved so much. For many months, he had not had any tantrums and followed school rules. Until Monday morning when he told his mother he didn't want to go to school anymore. Once there, he was completely out of control: refusing to do his work, running from class, and screaming.*
>
> The last day Fred was in school, his sitter was late picking him up. He had to wait in the office for half an hour, something that had never happened before. Now he was afraid to go back to school.
>
> Once Fred's mother understood why he had regressed, she sat with him and worked out a plan in case there was another time someone was going to be late picking him up. She explained to Fred that there are always people in the school office who will keep him safe and make sure he gets home.
>
> The next school day she went with him to school and they met with the office staff. They told Fred if someone didn't come to pick him up at his regular time, the teacher supervising pickup would bring him to the office. They showed him the place where children wait when someone is late for pickup.

Fred's mother had brought a book Fred liked and told him they would leave it in the pickup area in case he had to wait. She assured him even if his ride was late, he would get home and that everything would be alright.

She wrote out the steps Fred would follow if his ride was late and they read them over in the evening. They role played what he would do if his ride was late again. Even though Fred was improving, his mother continued this for several days. Fred soon felt safe at school again.

When this happens with neurotypical peers, they seem to understand they can rely on adults at their schools to make sure they get home and are reunited with their families. While they may be worried or upset, they usually do not develop intense fear.

I don't know exactly why some children with ASD become extremely upset when this happens, but I suspect it has to do with their Social Sense. When their routine is suddenly changed, they do not seem to know what will happen and become frightened. They do not have that instinctive understanding that the adults at the school will help them.

▶ CHILDREN WHO FEAR SCHOOL

There is another pattern of behavior that is even more challenging. These are ASD children who are very, very good in school. At home, however, they are absolutely terrified and beg their parents not to take them to school.

They may cry loudly and painfully in the morning before going to school and resist going in any way they can. They may cry themselves to sleep at night fearing the next day at school. Yet, when they walk to the schoolhouse door, they seemingly transform by magic. What their teachers see is a quiet, compliant child.

Parents who try to get assistance from their children's schools run into disbelief. Administrators and teachers listen to the parents pleas, look at the composed and compliant children, and wonder what is wrong with the parents. In fairness to the schools, it is very hard for school personnel to imagine the anguish of the parents of children with this problem.

> ***Billy's Fear***
>
> ***Billy had a wonderful year in kindergarten. When he began first grade, however, the teacher had a new behavior system. If the children were good their behavior marker was on green. If they started to have a problem, it changed to yellow as a warning. And, if the marker was moved to red, they were "in trouble."***
>
> ***Billy now seemed to be stressed when he went to school, but Billy's marker was always on green. Then one day when there was a substitute, she moved his marker to yellow because he had not finished his work on time. From that day forward Billy began to fear school.***

At school he was perfect, but at home his fear grew worse and worse. Billy would cry and beg not to go to school. He would struggle not to get out of the car to walk to class. But, as soon as he saw his teacher, his behavior completely changed and he walked quietly into the room.

Billy's mother asked his teacher to change the behavior system as it applied to Billy. His teacher did not want to do this, but after several meetings and descriptions of Billy's fear she relented. Billy was told he was so good that his teacher did not need the marker to be on the wall anymore and a reward system for good behavior was put in its place.

This problem typically is resolved as soon as the behavior system is changed. The main question teachers have about taking the marker off the wall is what to tell the other children. If they just tell the class that this child has a different system, I've never seen a problem. The rest of the class was told that Billy was going to use a different behavior system.

Where I've seen this pattern, it has been the result of the behavior management systems being used in the children's classrooms. Any type of behavior management system that introduces the threat of "getting in trouble" can trigger this response, but in my experience the green/yellow/red system seems to be the worst. Positive reward systems for good behavior are far more effective for children with ASD.

Sometimes there are meltdowns at school, but for the most part these children exhibit all their fear and anxiety at home. In the cases I've worked with, there is no solution except to remove the marker from the wall. Even if you tell your children the system will no longer apply to them, they continue to worry until it is no longer there.

I worked with one young boy who was told his marker would always stay green, but he continued to be stressed at home. The day we convinced the teacher to take the marker off the wall, he came home and said, "Thank God, it's gone."

Once again, I suspect this is a Social Sense problem. Neurotypical children know that "getting in trouble" means a telephone call home or a bad grade. They may not want to have that happen, but it is understandable and not frightening. For the ASD children who react with fear, it is my belief that "getting in trouble" is a concept they cannot understand, except that it is very, very bad. They are terrified of what is going to happen.

PART III
TOOLS TO CHANGE BEHAVIOR

CONSIDERATIONS FOR CHANGING BEHAVIOR

Children with ASD may need special encouragement to learn the rules of social interaction and to change their behavior. They need a lot of help to master the complicated rules needed to develop Social Insight. Just like learning history or science, learning to change a behavior requires focus and concentration.

There are many different ways to change behavior. Anything that works for your children is what you need to do. If you have a behavior system or a reward system that works, you should use it. If your behavior system uses consequences and it is working, don't change it now.

However, for many ASD children, behavior systems based on consequences don't work. In addition, not every reward system works for every child.

What to Request

A reward system only works if your children understand what you want them to do. The behaviors that are rewarded need to be clearly understood. Make sure not to use Social Meanings and Mislearned Words.

I have repeatedly run into individuals who do not want to use negatives to describe the behavior they want. For example, they don't want to write "don't curse" or "speak without cursing." They want to write "speak nicely." It is a whole lot easier to write a list of prohibited curse words, than to try to teach what "speak nicely" means.

Physical Limitations

Reward systems cannot work if you are requesting behaviors your children cannot do. If your children cannot sit for more than five minutes without standing up and walking around, there is no way to reward them into being able to sit for ten minutes.

The initial excitement of a reward sometimes allows children to suppress physical needs for a limited time. In the long run, however, physical needs will always win out - no matter how hard your children try. Make sure your children are able to do what you ask before beginning a reward system.

Learning and Attention Limitations

A reward cannot help your children learn new information. If your children do not understand a certain type of math, rewarding them for getting all their answers right will not help. While you can create a reward system to encourage attention, increasing the ability to pay attention requires other types of supports. Make sure to base rewards on things your children are able to do.

Rewards

A reward system cannot work if you are not offering rewards. One of the biggest problems I run into is that rewards that are offered to children are not what they want. **Rewards must be tailored to individual children.** Children who live for Thomas the Train cannot be rewarded with fancy pencils with random designs; however, they might do anything you ask for fancy pencils with Thomas the Train designs.

I have heard many teachers comment that ASD children in their classes do not care about going to the classroom prize box and do not respond to rewards. They don't respond to the rewards in the classroom prize box because there is nothing they want in the box.

For school, you may have to supply rewards that are attractive to your children or supplement school rewards at home. Giving a star or assigning points at school for a reward at home is the equivalent of receiving a reward at school. Once your children understand a point system, the points are the reward. They know they will be able to use the points to get what they want at home.

Reporting Systems

Some Reward Charts are really reporting systems, such as the "smiley face" chart. It has smiley faces for good behavior, neutral faces for acceptable behavior, and sad faces for unacceptable behavior.

If this is working for your children, there is no reason to change. However, for some children with ASD these charts are a disaster. The children completely ignore the smiley faces, obsess on the neutral and sad faces, and become stressed.

For many ASD children, Reward Charts work best when they show checkmarks or smiley faces or stars and nothing else. It is better to have the entire chart blank than to show a neutral or sad face.

Reward Charts

Don't become invested in using elaborate, decorated charts, stickers, special markers, or tokens. Because fancy charts, stickers, markers, or tokens can run out or be misplaced, I prefer very simple charts on regular paper that can be marked with a pencil. I have never seen a difference in how children respond to simple charts compared to fancy ones. In fact, the simple charts generally work better because the adults around the children are not as stressed about the charts.

Giving Rewards

Once children use the requested behavior, ALWAYS give them their reward - even if some other unacceptable behavior occurred. Let them know you are glad they earned their point, even though you are very disappointed about the other behavior. This is very difficult for many people - rewarding one behavior while dealing with another unacceptable behavior. However, for the rewards to be effective, your children need to be able to count on getting their rewards.

Once children use the correct behavior and points are given, NEVER take them away. It doesn't matter what awful things happened after the points are earned, never take away points. You can delay using points, but NEVER take them away.

Do not criticize your children when they fail to earn points. Let them know that it is okay and that they can try again the next day. If your children consistently fail to earn points, assuming the rewards are something they really want, you have selected behaviors they are unable to do.

Accumulating Reward Points

Points become a reward because your children can use them to get the things they want. Allowing your children to accumulate reward points can be very effective. They can spend their points on small items every day or they can hold on to the points until they add up to a bigger reward. Charts can be used both to show how many points have been accumulated and what the points can buy.

In order to use this type of system, your children must understand the mathematical concept known as correspondence. That is, if they are holding ten grapes and you ask for three grapes, they can give you three grapes.

The rewards your children can buy with their points must be things they really want, but they don't have to be expensive. Points can buy their choice of what you make for dinner or a special treat at the grocery store. Points can also buy extra television or computer time.

You can limit the choices or amount of time that can be used in one day or one week, just set the limit in advance so your children don't think you are being unfair.

If you use reward points for television or computer time, don't take away the time your children are currently allowed at the same time you begin a point system. If you plan to restrict their time and later use it as a reward, take it away at least a week before you introduce the reward system. Then when the reward system is introduced they will be happy they have a way to get more time.

Children should have some time they don't have to buy. Don't make them buy their favorite television program or stop all their computer activities. The anxiety this creates will likely interfere with their ability to learn the new behaviors you are requesting. You need to balance their normal access to these activities with the rewards that can give them more of what they want.

Money as a Reward

I am often asked if receiving money as a reward is appropriate. Since rewards have to be something that your children want, if your children want money, I think it is fine to use money as a reward. Just make sure that you set the rewards at amounts you can afford to pay.

TWO TYPES OF REWARD SYSTEMS

Intermittent Rewards

When psychologists study rewards, they look at different ways the subjects receive their reward. In one case, a reward may be given every single time a behavior occurs. In another case, a reward may be given after a set amount of time has passed, let's say every ten minutes, as long as the behavior occurred one or more times during that interval. Or, a reward can be intermittent.

An intermittent reward happens every now and then - there is no set schedule. This is the kind of reward gamblers receive when they play slot machines. Gamblers believe as long as they keep playing they will eventually get their reward.

Psychologists find that intermittent rewards are the most powerful rewards. When you first start to use an intermittent reward it should be fairly frequent. As the behavior you want increases, you can make the reward less frequent.

Catching Them Being Good

Some of the time, don't you just want to scream? Just when you really need some time to finish a project, the kids are squabbling and they keep running to you whining. It seems you just can't get anything done. Now, take a deep breath and set a timer for three minutes.

At the end of the three minutes, notice if there are any whining children surrounding you. If there aren't, find those children and praise them for what a good job they are doing. Be very specific - praise them for playing quietly, being nice to each other, or whatever.

Now, set your timer for five minutes. If there are no children crying near you, find them and tell them they are doing a good job. Set the timer for five more minutes and repeat the process again. Try your best to pay as little attention to them as possible if they come up to you before the time is up.

If they are doing well, increase the time to ten minutes, then to a half hour. Make sure to praise your children each time the timer goes off if they are "being good." Keep the timer at half an hour until they go to bed.

Beginning the next day, start with a half hour and work up to two hours. After that, just try to remember to randomly catch your children being good two or three times a day.

This is classic intermittent reinforcement. Most of the time, it works like a charm. Children want their parent's attention. They can get attention when they are annoying you or doing something they shouldn't be doing. Some attention, even negative attention, is better than no attention. Now, they can get your attention by being good. Of course, if your children are hungry, sleepy, or ill, this may not work.

Catching them being good gives them good attention which children prefer. This is one of my favorite behavior interventions and it works great for both ASD and neurotypical children.

Reward Charts

Reward Charts must clearly indicate how your children are progressing with their rewards.

> *Timmy's Troubles*
> *Timmy refused to close the door when he went to the bathroom; he would walk out of the bathroom with his pants down.*

Because Timmy was just learning to count, and does not yet understand the concept of correspondence, his Reward Chart must be very simple.

His mother had made a chart with ten spots for stickers. She told Timmy she would give him a sticker each time he went to the bathroom with the door closed and left it with his pants on. The chart carried over from one day to the next, so it was not hard for Timmy to eventually get ten stickers.

If Timmy made a mistake, his mother told him it was okay, he would have another chance to get a sticker.

> *Carl's Response*
> *Most of the time, Carl was a very verbal child; but, when his mother called his name, he did not respond. I suggested mom teach him to answer when she called his name. We chose the response "Yes?" and set up a Reward Chart.*

Carl's mother showed him his Reward Chart and told him he would get two points if he answered by himself or if he answered with one Reminder. If he needed more Reminders, he'd still get one point. Because Carl understands correspondence and addition, he was able to use a more advanced Reward Chart than Timmy and have a more complicated reward system.

Carl's rewards included:

Choice for Dinner	6 Points
Five Minutes of Computer Time	10 Points
Trip to McDonald's	30 Points
New Skateboard	75 Points

Carl's Reward Chart was simply a piece of notebook paper posted on the refrigerator where his mother could mark his points in pencil. When Carl used his points to buy rewards, she simply crossed off those points.

▶ LISTS

I use lists to help children have appropriate things to say and to do. Because they do not learn their behaviors instinctively, they often do not understand what we think are simple instructions or what words can make others uncomfortable.

Choice Lists

Your children may select words that are inappropriate. Sometimes there are unfortunate errors caused by misunderstanding the use of certain words. Lists of words can be used in many different ways to help your children know what to do and what to say.

Susan very much wanted to have friends. Unfortunately, she uses adult words instead of children's words when she meets new children. If you notice your children using adult words, you can use a Choice List to suggest children's words. Even with Everyday Learning, remember to explain the Social Sense concept that adults and children use different words.

This chart gives examples of adult words and examples of children's words. You need to help your children pick from the list of children's words, practice and role play. Like Susan, your children may need Reminders just before they meet new children.

Adult Words	Children's Words
You are so pretty.	Hey
You have beautiful hair	Want to play?

In developing lists it is very important to "get it right." That means you may have to ask neurotypical children to help you or to listen in on how children are speaking to each other. It is highly unlikely you would hear one child ask another, "How are you today?" It is important to use actual words and phrases that your children's friends and classmates use.

Embarrassed many times when she had attended funerals with Simon, Frieda taught him appropriate phrases to use and cautioned him not to use any other words. She made him lists with appropriate phrases such as: "I'm so sorry." "I miss him too." "This is a difficult time."

Frieda was using a Choice List when she gave Simon the words to say at a funeral. Simon was not able to come up with his own phrases because he does not have Theory of Mind. He cannot predict what might make someone else feel uncomfortable. With the

Choice List Frieda provided, Simon had specific appropriate things he could choose from.

Check First Lists

Another important use of lists is providing guidance to help develop Social Sense. Especially as ASD children get older, they may have difficulty understanding what topics are and are not appropriate. A topic that is appropriate in one setting may not be appropriate in another setting.

It is important to give your children the opportunity to express their ideas, but we don't want them to get in trouble.

> **Kenny comments on personal appearance, race, religion, and many other topics have repeatedly gotten him in trouble at school. Kenny's check first list includes: race, ethnicity, religion, sex, politics, body odors, private parts, and physical appearance.**

Kenny has been told he can talk about race, religion, and politics in his Government Class, as long as he only talks about the aspects of these subjects that the class is discussing.

Lists of words or subjects can be very helpful for children with ASD. They can take the guesswork out of dealing with difficult or personal topics that can get them in a lot of trouble.

Because you should never stop your children from raising legitimate concerns, these lists come with specific instructions. As the name implies, these are lists to remind your children to "check first" before talking about these topics. Discussing the topics on a Check First List must be allowed with a family member, a safe person, the family doctor, or other trusted adults.

All children must be able to discuss their concerns over matters related to sex, ethnicity, race, religion, bodily functions, and so on. Because your children cannot always judge when certain words or topics are appropriate, however, they should not discuss them without clear guidelines.

Prohibited Lists

Another use of lists is to help your children understand what kinds of things they should and should not do or say. Sometimes there is the intentional use of offensive or emotional words because children with ASD want to fit in or get a reaction from others.

Remember Brett? He was in trouble in kindergarten for doing and saying inappropriate things - things that he did not get in trouble for at home. Brett's mother used two different lists to help Brett understand the things he should not do at school.

One list told Brett what behaviors were prohibited at school. The list used his own words to describe his behavior.

Any kind of "playing around" is not allowed at school.

No acting like a Power Ranger
No Tae Kwon Do
No biting or scratching
No hitting or punching
No choking or hugging (wrestling holds)

The other list told Brett what words he was not to use at school.

Certain words are not allowed at school.

Jerk
Loser
Double loser
Stupid
I'm going to kick your butt

Even though Brett could not read, having his words written down made more of an impact than if they were just repeated to him. In addition, when his mother reviewed his Behavior Lesson, she was sure she was not leaving anything out.

Kenny also had to have a prohibited list. In addition to not understanding topics that were inappropriate, he understands the meanings of words based on their dictionary definitions, rather than their emotional impact.

> **Kenny understands liar as someone who makes a false statement and stupid as someone who is not smart. He uses these words just like any other word to describe other people. He does not understand the emotional impact of these words. Whenever Kenny uses a word that has a negative emotional impact, his mother discusses the word and puts it on his prohibited list.**

Without these lists, it is likely Brett and Kenny would not have learned what they could and could not say and do. You cannot expect your children to understand which words are inappropriate without specific lists and instructions. This is especially the case since many of the words they use are words they hear at school - words that don't seem to get other children in trouble.

AUTHOR'S NOTE

The most important part of Social Insight is helping your children to understand there are components to social behavior that can be learned. This is the first step to being able to teach Social Insight. The concepts of Social Actions, Social Words, Social Settings, Social Signals, and Social Sense are integral parts of our social world. Without this initial understanding, the social world is frequently a very confusing place for our children.

As you become aware that you learned many of your social skills instinctively, and that your children cannot, you may be less frustrated and more able to offer guidance. In fact, just by becoming aware, you will be better equipped to help your children. What confused you before – but it's just common sense – will now make more sense.

There are very different levels of ability in actually learning these concepts, but any level of understanding can enrich the lives of the children learning these new ideas. In fact, as you have seen in a number of examples in this book, many adults can also benefit from this instruction.

It is my hope that professionals in the field of autism, with far more knowledge than I possess, will become more aware of the need for this type of instruction. While practicing specific skills is very valuable, it is important for your children to have a context in which to put those skills.

By having names for the component parts of social interactions, children who are confused by social interactions may be able to put them into some context.

It is my sincere hope that your children will benefit from the information presented in this book.

GLOSSARY

Behavior Lessons

These are structured lessons that include five specific elements. Replacement Behaviors are what is substituted for the behavior you are trying to change. Social Sense is helping your child understand why you are changing the behavior. A Reminder is help to remember what to do. A Reward is the incentive for doing what you are asking. Teaching Time is the process of teaching your children to engage in the new behavior.

Cognitive Meltdowns

Some children with ASD experience cognitive meltdowns. When I use this term, I am talking about children who actually lose the ability to understand directions when they are upset. They are not really able to process what you are saying to them or what you want them to do once in a meltdown.

Everyday Learning

The general interaction you have with your children on a regular basis; where you take opportunities to teach about what is happening around them or ways to change their behavior to be more successful.

Literal Language

When your children respond to the literal meaning of what someone has said rather than what they meant.

Mislearned Words

These are words that are being used in a way that is not typical. It is fairly common for some ASD children to learn to follow a rule only for a specific word. So a child may learn the rule in school is not to hit, but not understand that the exact same Action given a different name is the same thing.

Private Behavior

ASD children need to be taught from a very young age that certain behaviors should only occur when they are alone. While these behaviors fit more than one category, our main concern here is with their effect as Social Signals. Nose picking and touching private parts fall into this category.

Regress

When children go back to a previous, inappropriate behavior, they are regressing.

Replacement Behavior

The behavior you are substituting for the unwanted behavior you are trying to change.

Reward

The incentive to learn and use a new response is a reward. ***Rewards can be anything that your children like.***

Rumbling Phase

The behaviors you observe before a full meltdown occurs.

Scripting

Children repeat memorized scripts throughout the day.

Self-Talk

Children repeat their thoughts out loud.

Social Actions

These are behaviors that happen during a social interaction. It is what we normally think of as social behavior - the general things we do. These are what a teacher normally tells you when they describe an incident with your child.

Social Errors

This is the general term for the errors your children make in social interactions.

Social Insight

When all the components fall into place and a child with an Autism Spectrum Disorder learns to predict and understand social behavior. It is the comprehension that social interactions are made up of distinct parts that can be studied and understood at various levels. It is how we understand and implement unstated rules of behavior.

Social Meanings

The meanings given to words that have a whole group of behaviors included in their meanings. For example, teachers sometimes tell their students to "pay attention," but want them to sit up without speaking or fidgeting and to keep their eyes on the teacher.

Social Sense

This is why we should behave in a certain way in a social interaction. Your children need to think about the reasons they are engaged in a particular social interaction. Social Sense can also tell us why other people are doing what they do.

Social Setting

This is where and with whom a social interaction occurs. It includes the place and the people.

Social Signals

How someone engages in social interactions to give those interactions specific meanings. They include aspects of behavior that help us decide what Social Actions and Social Words really mean.

Social Words

Words used during an interaction. Social Words may have meanings that do not coincide with their dictionary definitions, causing your children to become confused.

Teaching Time

Structured time allocated to teaching a new behavior or explaining a new concept.

www.ingramcontent.com/pod-product-compliance
Lightning Source LLC
Chambersburg PA
CBHW050906160426
43194CB00011B/2312